<small>PRAISE FOR</small>

devotion

A *NEW YORK TIMES BOOK REVIEW* EDITORS' CHOICE

"Shapiro is a thoughtful observer, and her writing is lovely. Some of her most vivid scenes are those in which she brings other people to life: her mother sitting through a therapy session in a froth of rage, holding X-rays of a lethal brain tumor that she doesn't disclose; her father at his morning prayers."
—*Washington Post*

"I was immensely moved by this elegant book, which reminded me all over again that all of us—at some point or another—must buck up our courage and face down the big spiritual questions of life, death, love, loss, and surrender. Dani Shapiro probes all those questions gracefully and honestly, avoiding overly simple conclusions, while steadfastly exploring her own complicated relationship to faith and doubt."
—Elizabeth Gilbert, author of *Eat, Pray, Love*

"Lyrical. . . . Shapiro is a gifted chronicler of frayed nerves. . . . With *Devotion*, Shapiro joins the ranks of . . . Kathleen Norris's *Cloister Walk*, Anne Lamott's *Traveling Mercies*, and, of course, Elizabeth Gilbert's *Eat, Pray, Love*."
—*New York Times Book Review*

"Eloquently told and unflinchingly honest."
—Jeannette Walls, author of *Half Broke Horses* and *The Glass Castle*

"If Elizabeth Gilbert's *Eat, Pray, Love* was about the fantasy of a spiritual journey, Dani Shapiro's *Devotion* is about the reality. . . . Shapiro's modesty and her persistence are admirable. . . . Also touching is her gratitude toward those of all faiths who have helped her along the way." —*Columbus Dispatch*

"An insightful and penetrating memoir that readers will instantly identify with. . . . Absorbing, intimate, direct, and profound, Shapiro's memoir is a satisfying journey that will touch fans and win her plenty of new ones." —*Publishers Weekly* (starred review)

"Shapiro movingly unravels her personal history. . . . [Her] spiritual inquiry digs at doubts many of us face about our place in the universe, and her struggles with the God question serve as a hopeful reminder that a belief system can begin with an individual manifesto." —*Elle*

"What makes *Devotion* most compelling is its willingness to explore the elusiveness of certainty." —*Time*

"I was on the verge of tears more than once in the course of Dani Shapiro's impeccably structured spiritual odyssey. But *Devotion*'s biggest triumph is its voice: funny and unpretentious, concrete and earthy—appealing to skeptics and believers alike. This is a gripping, beautiful story."

—Jennifer Egan, author of *A Visit from the Goon Squad* and *The Keep*

"Shapiro's journey is a deeply reflective one, and her struggles are as complex as they are insightful, philosophical, and universally human." —*Booklist*

"The one book that anyone over, say, thirty-five needs to read right now." —Jesse Kornbluth, *The Huffington Post*

"A beautiful, wry, and moving story about one intelligent woman's journey into her own life, to the corners where intelligence doesn't always help. *Devotion* is a book for anyone who knows or suspects that they are, to paraphrase Carl Jung, thoroughly unprepared to step into the afternoon of life." —Amy Bloom, author of *Away*

"Shapiro's *Devotion* ranks with the best." —*Library Journal*

devotion

Also by Dani Shapiro

FICTION

Black & White
Family History
Picturing the Wreck
Fugitive Blue
Playing with Fire

NONFICTION

Slow Motion

devotion

•

A MEMOIR

Dani Shapiro

HARPER ⬤ PERENNIAL

NEW YORK • LONDON • TORONTO • SYDNEY • NEW DELHI • AUCKLAND

HARPER ◉ PERENNIAL

A hardcover edition of this book was published in 2010 by HarperCollins Publishers.

P.S.™ is a trademark of HarperCollins Publishers.

HarperCollins books may be purchased for educational, business, or sales
promotional use. For information please e-mail the Special Markets Department
at SPsales@harpercollins.com.

FIRST HARPER PERENNIAL EDITION PUBLISHED 2011.

Designed by Jennifer Daddio/Bookmark Design & Media Inc.

The Library of Congress has catalogued the hardcover edition as follows:
Shapiro, Dani.
    Devotion / Dani Shapiro.—1st ed.
        p. cm.
    ISBN 978-0-06-162834-4
    1. Shapiro, Dani.   2. Shapiro, Dani—Religion.   3. Novelists, American—
20th century—Biography.   4. Jewish women—United States—Biography.   5. Faith.
6. Prayer.   7. Devotion.   8. Shapiro, Dani—Family.   I. Title
    PS3569.H3387Z463   2010
    818'.5403—dc22
    [B]
                                                                    2009024816

ISBN 978-0-06-162835-1 (pbk.)

    19   20   LSC   10   9   8   7   6   5   4

For Michael and Jacob

Being human cannot be borne alone. We need other presences. We need soft night noises—a mother speaking downstairs, a grandfather rumbling in response, cars swishing past on Philadelphia Avenue and their headlights wheeling around the room. We need the little clicks and signs of a sustaining otherness. We need the Gods.

—JOHN UPDIKE

I.

A woman named Sandra was cradling my head in her hands. We were in a small room—just the two of us—and it was so quiet I could hear the ticking of her watch. The air smelled faintly of eucalyptus. A high window overlooked a parking lot, and beyond the parking lot, mountains. I tried to relax—that was the point, wasn't it?—but I wasn't relaxed at all. I had signed up for something called Master Level Energy Work, thinking it would be like a massage. But this was no massage. For one thing, she was sighing a lot.

After some moments, she spoke. "I see some sort of teacher. Do you have teachers in your life?"

"Yes." A few people came to mind: a man in his seventies who had a shock of white hair and wore baggy suits; another man, younger, with a closely trimmed dark beard; a tiny gray-haired woman, also in her seventies.

"Do they assume a form? How do they appear to you?"

I hadn't realized talking would be involved. Had I known, I never would have made the appointment. I wanted to lie still and be silent; it was peace I was after. I had been waking up in a cold sweat nearly every night, my heart pounding. I paced my house, worried about . . . well, worried about everything.

"Your teachers . . . ," Sandra prodded.

"Well, sometimes we have coffee," I said. "Or we exchange e-mail."

"But what do the forms look like? Do you see a light? Do they seem . . . spectral?"

Ah. She meant *otherworldly* teachers. Beneath my closed lids, I rolled my eyes. This wasn't going to work for me, this talk of spirits. I started wondering how long I had been lying there, and how much longer this process was going to take. Would she be insulted if I got up and left? I was twitchy, impatient. Disappointed, too. It was rare that I allowed myself such a self-indulgent, not to mention expensive, hour.

She sighed again, a bit more loudly.

"Are you feeling . . . pushed?" she asked. "Like someone's pushing you from behind?"

That precise feeling had been plaguing me for as long as I could remember.

"Yes," I said. "Exactly."

I was always racing. I couldn't settle down. I mean, I was *settled down*—I was happily married and the mother of an eight-year-old boy. But I often felt a sense of tremendous urgency, as if there was a whip at my back. I was fleeing something—but what?

Her hands on my neck began to tremble.

"It's your father," she said. "Your father is pushing you."

Had I told her about my father? No. I thought about what she might have gleaned from looking at me: blond woman, mid-forties; wedding band; tank watch; yoga clothes; a necklace dangling with two charms, M and J. How could she have known that my father was dead? Did I have a "tell," like a poker player?

"Was your father a religious man? A man of faith?"

She said it as if she already knew the answer and was only waiting for my confirmation. I was suddenly very alert.

"Yes, he was very religious."

"And you have a young son?"

"I do." She had a fifty-fifty shot of getting that right. The charm necklace was a giveaway that I probably had at least one child. I relaxed a little.

The trembling in Sandra's hands grew more pronounced.

"Your father apologizes. He's a very gentle spirit."

A stillness settled over me, gauzy and soft. I wasn't frightened, not exactly. Sandra's fingers were hot against my neck. I pictured my father. His sweet round face. His kind, hazel-green eyes behind rimless glasses. His easy smile. *Hiya, darling!* I could summon his voice—always a bit louder than he meant it to be—as surely as if I just heard it yesterday. *How's my girl?*

"Your father is trying to help you," Sandra said. "That's why you feel pushed. He wants to share with you what he believes. He didn't get a chance to—"

She broke off. Another heaving sigh.

"Is there anything you want to say to your father?"

I tried to remember what Sandra looked like: around sixty, reddish hair, a weathered face. Ordinary. Like she might be standing in front of me on line at the supermarket, rather than behind me, her hands on my skull. What was happening between us defied everything I believed, but I had entered a place beyond belief. I was here now. On the other side of logic. In a place that felt true, if not quite real.

"That I miss him," I said. My own voice sounded strange and

far away. I was weightless, tumbling. Tears began to leak from the corners of my eyes. They soaked my hairline, but I didn't move an inch. Even if my father wasn't in the room, it was the closest I had been to him in twenty years.

"He died when I was young, and everything I am—everything I've become since that day—is because of him. Because I had to make his death mean something."

Sandra moved her hands slightly to the left.

"He acknowledges that," she said.

She rocked my head from side to side.

"Your father is asking if you want him to stay."

"Yes." I was weeping now. My father didn't live long enough to know my husband or son. It was my greatest sorrow. "Yes, I want him to stay."

2.

Jacob ran ahead of us toward the wooded banks of the Shepaug River, holding a hunk of bread in his small hands. The air was soft, the sun strong. It was a hot Indian-summer afternoon in the middle of September. Lazy, drunken bees hovered all around. The river seemed more like a creek, the water trickling slowly around dark gray rocks glittering in the brightness.

There were perhaps twenty of us—mostly people I didn't know—our heels crunching the dried leaves and twigs as we made our way to the water's edge. In this Connecticut nature preserve where horse trailers lined the parking lot, where the prep school track team trained in the hills, we must have been an odd sight: an assortment of adults and children, dressed more nicely than a walk in the country would seem to call for, carrying bits of bread.

It was the first day of Rosh Hashanah, and many years had passed since I had last set foot in a synagogue, much less participated in this ritual called *tashlich*, which follows the long Rosh Hashanah service. I dragged myself to the Shepaug River, fighting my own resistance every step of the way. I had better things to do. Virtually *anything* seemed like a better thing to do. I could have stayed home and organized my closets. But no—I was here. And not only had I come, but I had somehow managed—some might call it a miracle—to drag my husband and son with me.

Tamara, the spiritual leader (not a rabbi) of this loosely formed coalition (it's not a congregation) of Jews, gathered us around her with quiet authority. She wore a yarmulke on her short-cropped black hair. The first time I saw her, I thought she was a yeshiva boy studying for his bar mitzvah. She passed around copies of the *tashlich* verse from Samuel 7:6 and we read aloud, our voices lost in the vastness of the forest, the trees towering over our heads.

Who is like You, God, who removes iniquity and overlooks transgression of the remainder of His inheritance. He doesn't remain angry forever because He desires kindness. He will return and He will be merciful to us, and He will conquer our iniquities, and He will cast them into the depths of the seas.

Which is why we were there, on the banks of the Shepaug. To cast our sins into a moving body of water by tossing our bits of bread into the slow-moving trickle until it carried them all away. Sins, be gone. The Shepaug flows into Lake Lillinonah, a dammed portion of the Housatonic River. I pictured small, sodden, radioactive morsels floating downstream, infused with each of our sins, one by one disintegrating in the depths of the lake. I looked around: a local real estate developer had moved off to the side and was standing very still, his lips moving. A mom from Jacob's school stared intently at the trickling water, then hurled a piece of bread as far as she could.

I joined Jacob at the riverbank, and stood next to him in silence. My own piece of bread was warm and moist in my palm. In the car, on the way here, I had tried to explain to him what we were doing; why he wasn't in school, and instead was wearing an uncomfortable blazer and long pants on this hot September day. But I hadn't done a very good job of it.

"What's a sin?" Jacob now asked.

It was one of those Mommy-needs-to-get-it-right questions. There had been so many of them, lately; so many questions that felt like tests of my own mettle. *Where is God? Does he exist? How come I can't see him? Can he see me?*

"Sin is a big word," I said. "Why don't we think of it as things we feel bad about, that we want to let go of. Things we'd like to do better in the coming year."

Even as the words came out of my mouth, they felt inadequate. I was a phony. Play-acting the part of a spiritually inclined, or at least Jewishly inclined, wife and mother who had cajoled her husband and son into their good clothes so that we could enact a ritual so distant from our daily lives that we might as well have been kneeling at a Buddhist temple, or Catholic church, or wherever people kneel the world over.

I fought the urge to flee—an urge that was often with me,

these days. Instead, I closed my eyes and breathed in the lingering summer warmth, the sharp scent of the river.

Please.

With a single word, I felt hot tears backing up. I was instantly lost in the place I always found myself during the rare times I summoned up the nerve to reach back and grasp for a bit of the tradition I grew up with. Numb, weepy, deeply alive, fighting it, fighting *myself* and the long line of ancestors waiting their turn, there to tell me that no matter how I'd like to think otherwise, this sunny day at the river was important. I could practically see them: old men with skullcaps and beards. Unsmiling women with huge bosoms and dark, tightly pulled-back hair.

I tossed a few crumbs in. I wanted to make it last.

Please. Help me to understand.

It would have been so much easier not to come. If we hadn't come here today, Jacob would have been in third-grade Spanish, I would have been at my desk working on a magazine assignment, or maybe reading a student's manuscript. Michael would have been at his office down the road, also sitting at his desk, working on a screenplay or procrastinating by reading the latest political blogs. A normal day. A normal assimilated day in our normal assimilated lives—lives that had nothing to do with ancient texts and metaphors as dusty and old-fashioned as the photographs of those very same solemn ancestors in their Eastern European shtetl that line the walls of our basement rec room.

I want to do better.

The words were coming to me unforced, unbidden. *Do better.* The list of things I wanted to do better at was as long as the Shepaug River itself. I wanted be a better mother, wife, writer, teacher, person, member of society. I definitely wanted to sleep better. Oh, and eat better, have more patience, drink more water. I wanted to practice yoga more days of the week. I wanted to understand the difference between the Sunnis and the Shiites. I wanted to be someone who not only bought flaxseed oil at the health food store, but actually ingested it. There was no end to my desire for self-improvement. But was this what I meant?

I glanced over at Michael, who was standing on a large rock jutting out over the river, and was surprised to see that my husband was holding a piece of bread and appeared to be—was it possible?—involved in what was going on. He didn't have that bored, going-through-the-motions look on his face that I knew so well in other circumstances, and would have expected to see in these. He was focused, thoughtful. Casting away his sins.

"Do we have to go?" he had asked me earlier that morning, sounding a bit like he must have when he was fourteen. "I can't find my belt. Christ! My suit doesn't fit."

Jacob squeezed his eyes shut and tossed the first bit of bread into the water. *Things you want to let go of.* A school of silvery minnows darted around the bread as it floated downstream.

"Can I tell you what I wished for, Mommy?"

"Oh, honey, it's not supposed to be a—"

But then I stopped. What was the difference, really? What was the desire to let something go, if not a wish?

"I wished for that remote-controlled helicopter," Jacob said. "The one I saw on TV."

I looked at my little blond-haired, blue-eyed boy in his navy blue blazer and khakis. He looked more like a Ralph Lauren ad than a kid at High Holiday services. He was a thoroughly modern child. A Jewish boy who barely knew he was Jewish, who believed in Santa, who had never heard of the Holocaust, who had—as a two-year-old—been playing with a tower of wooden blocks when we heard the sound of the first plane crashing into the World Trade Center a mile away. A boy who was now being raised in bucolic New England, in the land of white churches and village greens.

Please. The word came to me once more. It seemed to emerge from some deep and hollow cavern. I threw my last morsel of bread away, then turned from the river.

3.

I had reached the middle of my life and knew less than I ever had before. Michael, Jacob, and I lived on top of a hill, surrounded by old trees, a vegetable garden, stone walls. From the outside, things looked pretty good. But deep inside myself, I had begun to quietly fall apart. Nights, I quivered in the darkness like a wounded animal. Something was very wrong, but I didn't know what it was. All I knew was that I felt terribly anxious and unsteady. *Doomed.* Each morning I drove Jacob down a dirt road to his sweet little school. We all got yearly physicals. Our well water was tested for contaminants. Nothing—absolutely nothing I could put my finger on—was the matter. Except that I was often on the verge of tears. Except that it seemed that there had to be more than this hodgepodge of the everyday. Inside each joy was a hard kernel of sadness, as if I was always preparing myself for impending loss.

Beneath the normal routine of my life—the school functions and lunch boxes and Little League games and family dinners—all was churning, random, chaos. We'd had a close call when Jacob was an infant—a scary time—but that was behind us now. Wasn't it? Still, I couldn't stop thinking. What was going to keep bad things from happening: a tree branch from falling, an electrical wire from coming loose, a cluster of cells from mutating, a speeding baseball from slamming into a small, vulnerable head? Was there no pattern, no wisdom, no plan?

I had put off thinking about this, because it seemed that there would always be time. Later, in a few years, I would turn my attention to the big questions—once I had taken care of the smaller ones. Except the smaller ones just kept coming. And gradually— though it felt like a split second—I realized that I had reached the still point at the very top of a curve. I'm not much for roller coasters, but now I felt like I was on one. It had been so slow, going up. But the ride from here on in was going to be impossibly fast. Had I lived half my life? More? Sometimes I looked at Jacob's lanky legs, his growing-boy body slung across the sofa, and saw with aching clarity that eight years had gone by since we'd swaddled him in his infant seat and brought him home from the hospital. *It all goes so quickly*, every parent says. *Take in every single minute.* This is always offered as a piece of wistful advice, because of course it's not possible to take in every minute. It's hard to take in even a single minute.

I needed to place my faith in *something*. I didn't want our family's life to speed by in a blur of meals, schools, camps, barbecues, picnics, vacations—each indistinguishable from the next. I wanted to slow it down—to find ways to infuse our lives with greater depth and meaning. My own childhood had been spent steeped in religious ritual. There were rules for eating, speaking, sleeping, praying. I never knew *why* we did what we did—it was simply the way it was. I had fled this at the earliest opportunity, but replaced it with nothing. I wasn't exactly a nonbeliever. Nor was I a believer. Where did that leave me? Anxious, fearful, lonely, resentful, depressed—troubled by a powerful and, some would say, deeply irreverent sense of futility.

Most nights, when I stretched out next to Jacob on his narrow bed with a few books balanced on my stomach, he had other plans. He wanted to talk about what happens when we die. His questions had been coming fast and furious. He wanted answers—his voice piercingly clear and pure. "I don't want to die," he'd say. And then: "What happens? Where do we go?"

"Well . . ." I played for time. "Some people believe that we come back in another life. It's called reincarnation."

"You mean, I could come back as a dog?"

"No, I don't think so. Probably not. Probably as a person."

I watched his delicate profile as he digested this information.

"And other people believe there's a heaven. That we go to heaven when we die."

I left hell out of it, since I was cherry-picking anyway.

"And other people think that the soul continues to exist," I went on, feeling his small, beating heart pressed against my arm as he lay on his side. "That we stay alive when people remember us."

"Like Grandma?" he asked.

My mother had died when Jacob was four. He would have few memories of her. And none of my father. None at all.

"Yes," I answered. "Like Grandma. And your grandpa, too. I think about them every day."

But when it came to a deeper response to Jacob's questions, I was failing him and I knew it. I was laying out a smorgasbord of options, but I wasn't telling him what *I* believe—because I truly didn't know. Each day, e-mails I had signed up for kept appearing in my in-box—*My Daily Om, Weekly Kabbalah Consciousness Tune-up* —like the results of a Rorschach test: spiritually confused wife and mother in midlife, seeking answers. For years, I had dabbled: little bite-size morsels of Buddhism, the Yoga Sutra, Jewish mysticism. I had a regular yoga practice, but often felt like I was only scratching the surface. My bookshelves were filled with books I had bought with every good intention, important books containing serious insights about how to live. Over the years, they remained unopened. Taking up space.

What would happen if I opened the books? If I opened *myself*—as an adventurer, an explorer into the depths of every single day? What if—instead of fleeing—I were to continue to quiver in the darkness? It wasn't so much that I was in search of answers. In fact, I was wary of the whole idea of answers. I wanted to climb all the way inside the questions and see what was there.

4.

Here we come a-wassailing among the leaves so green! Here we come a-wand'ring, so fair to be seen!

The first, second, and third graders filed into the theater and onto the bleachers for the Winter Solstice concert. Parents were crammed into the theater's seats, some still wrapped in their winter coats. Eric, an emergency room doctor, Liz, a landscape architect, Denise, an attorney, Darren, a software designer. I was friendly with many of them, but still I always had to brace myself for these school events. I felt cut off from the other parents, as if they lived in a country to which I had been denied entry.

Love and joy come to you, and to you your wassail too, and God bless you and send you a happy new year, and God send you a happy new year.

As Jacob climbed the bleachers to the second riser, his eyes scanned the audience in the dark, searching us out. Like the other boys, he was dressed in a white button-down shirt and black pants. The girls had gotten a bit more creative: leggings under skirts, black Mary Janes with white lacy socks. Jacob spotted us, tilted his head to the side, and gave us a distinctly Jacob-like smile, both bashful and proud.

We are not daily beggars who beg from door to door, but we are neighbors' children whom you have seen before . . .

Jacob looked straight ahead, arms loose by his sides; his voice was clear and distinct to my ears, even among seventy-five others. And suddenly—why hadn't I expected this?—a rumbling rose up from deep within me. It was familiar, unstoppable—an avalanche. I knew I had to sit there and let the rocks fly. If any of the other parents happened to glance in my direction, they would never have known from looking at me. Outside, I was composed—serene, even. But inside, all hell had broken loose. It was the daytime version of my nightly panic. I knew that I couldn't fight it; resisting only made it worse.

We almost lost him.

It was all I could do not to whisper it out loud. To put my hand on the shoulder of the mom next to me, or the one in front, or behind. None of them knew this thing that defined me, the knowledge I wore like an invisible cloak. *We almost lost him.* I leaned into Michael and wondered if he was thinking about it too. Would we ever sit in an audience and watch Jacob do normal little-boy things—swing a bat, recite lines in a play, sing in a holiday concert—without having the thought? *We almost lost him.* Repeating it was like a prayer, a mantra. It was my own personal covenant. I could never allow myself to forget, even in the happiest times. *Especially* in the happiest times. It was a private bargain I had struck—but with whom?

I was always compiling lists in my mind: what *had* gone wrong, what *could* go wrong. I hadn't figured how to live with my heightened awareness of exactly how fragile it all is. And so the lists grew and grew. I was trying to control the universe—and it's hard work to try to control the universe. I thought that maybe by naming each potential disaster, I could prevent it. Michael could have a heart attack shoveling snow. Lightning could hit our house. The superstitions I grew up with—Yiddish terms, peasant language left over from the Old World—rose up from some buried place. *Poo, poo, poo.* I warded off the evil eye like a fishwife. *K'ayn ayn hora.* I counted to eighteen, *chai*, the Hebrew number signifying life. Eighteen, for the number of seconds I microwaved my morning coffee. Eighteen, for the number of crunches I did at the end of my yoga practice. Eighteen, so that the angel of death might pass over our house for another day.

5.

Just a few months ago, Michael and Jacob had been driving home late at night from a baseball game when someone threw a glass bottle of salad dressing off an embankment. The bottle hit the roof of our car and shattered. One fraction of a second earlier, and it would have hit the windshield.

Salad dressing, I thought to myself, when Michael told me what had happened. I never considered salad dressing.

6.

Maybe books weren't enough. Maybe I needed to travel to some far-flung place, though it didn't feel very practical. Thoreau may have lived in isolation, but I lived in Connecticut. I drove carpool, ordered socks by the dozen from Land's End, paid the mortgage, filed health insurance claims, gave dinner parties, supported my local congressman. I worried about bills, and was drowning in Post-its: *Michael, colonoscopy. J—dentist!* The lists fluttered everywhere. They were attached to the edges of my desk, the pages of my appointment book, the kitchen counter. I was mired in the domesticity that I loved—that same domesticity that kept me on a treadmill from the first sounds of pounding feet in the morning to the last hazy thought—*We're almost out of dog food*—that drifted through my mind before passing out at night. Could I find and hold on to a deeper truth than the whir and strum of my daily life, which seemed designed to ensure that some day I would wake up—after the years of packed lunches and piano practice and rushed dinners—and wonder where it all had gone?

I told myself that I could sort this out—right here, from the central command station of my life. What good would it do me if the answers ended up being *out there*? I wasn't out there! And what's more, I knew that anything I might learn by going away would disappear in a flash once I was back home, sorting the dry cleaning from the laundry. I wasn't in a *shala*, or a *zendo*, or a shrine, or temple. I was here in my house—and I needed to figure out how to work with what I had.

After all, some of my greatest moments of clarity—those little eureka moments of truth—had happened in unlikely places: wheeling a cart down a supermarket aisle, driving along an empty stretch of highway, lying in bed next to Jacob as he drifted off to sleep. And I knew from my yoga practice that those insights are already fully formed—they're literally inside our bodies, if only we know where to look. Yogis use a beautiful Sanskrit word, *sam-*

skara, to describe the knots of energy that are locked in the hips, the heart, the jaw, the lungs. Each knot tells a story—a narrative rich with emotional detail. Release a *samskara* and you release that story. Release your stories, and suddenly there is more room to breathe, to feel, to experience the world.

I wanted to release my stories and find what was beneath them—I wanted to work with the raw materials of my life—but I wasn't sure how to do it. I felt like I was sweeping these ideas and concerns, like dust motes, into the corners of my days.

8 a.m.: school dropoff
9:30–11:30: magazine deadline
12:00–3:00: spiritual awakening
3:15: school pickup
3:30–4:30: piano lesson
5:00–7:00: more deep inquiry
7:00: dinner on the table

No—I quickly realized—I needed help. A jump start. I needed company, fellow sojourners. I needed teachers. And maybe this was where the *shala*s, the *zendo*s, the shrines and temples, came in. But I had never been much of a joiner. At the edges of any group—from the playgrounds of my childhood to the cocktail parties of my adulthood—I always felt like an outsider, my nose pressed to the glass. And anyway, where was I supposed to go? And when? And who would take care of my family? They might go naked, not to mention unshowered, and eventually starve to death without my constant presence. And besides, I didn't like groups. And I needed a private bathroom. And I was afraid I'd be homesick. Did I say I'm not much of a joiner?

Still, most mornings—between the highly evolved practice of checking the Amazon sales ranking of my latest novel and lustfully tracking down an unaffordable pair of stiletto-heeled Jimmy Choo boots—I found myself on the Web site of Kripalu, a yoga and meditation center in the Berkshire Hills of western Massachusetts. It was only a ninety-minute drive from my house. I studied Kripalu's calendar for a retreat that didn't strike me as too scary. "The Ecstasy of Sound: A Music and Healing Workshop" sounded way too woo-woo. As did "The Masks of the Goddess: Ritual, Theatre and Stories of the Sacred Feminine." I was highly suspicious of the smiling people with their gray, kinky hair, loose yoga pants, and Birkenstock sandals. They looked like they had migrated directly from Woodstock. Who were they? Could they possibly be as contented as they appeared to be? I couldn't imagine what it would be like to join them. I put up all kinds of roadblocks, conducting endless loopy conversations with myself.

Who are you kidding? You can't do this.

Why not?

It isn't you.

Well, whatever me is, it isn't working.

What do you want?

More. *I want more.*

So what you're saying is—

I'm not sure. But I want to go deeper.

Deeper into what?

But then something would disrupt the train of thought. A UPS truck heading up the driveway. The new puppy at the door, scratching to get out. An urgent e-mail from a student. A phone call from a fact-checker. And the next thing I knew, I was back in the thick of it. My rich, busy, over-full life—speeding by.

7.

When I was little, I used to sit and watch my father as he set out to say his morning prayers. In the den of our house in Hillside, he would face east—past the swimming pool, past the forsythia hedge that separated our yard from the next-door neighbors', past the New Jersey Turnpike, all the way to Jerusalem. Dressed in his suit pants, shirt, and tie, he took his tallit from its blue velvet pouch, gently shook out its folds, and wrapped it around himself like a shawl. It was an old, well-made tallit, yellowed over time. Its fringe, the tzitzit, was soft and knotted. Perhaps this was the same tallit he had received on his bar mitzvah. Or maybe it had belonged to my grandfather, who had died when I was an infant. I never asked, and so I never knew.

Once the tallit was in place, it was time for the tefillin. My father half sang, half murmured the blessing on laying tefillin as he very precisely placed the first phylactery—a small, perfectly square black box—on his left bicep, exactly two finger breadths above his elbow joint. He then placed the second phylactery high on his forehead, like a miner's light. He had been laying tefillin every weekday morning of his life since he was thirteen, so he didn't have to measure—they were like extensions of his body. He began to bind: around his arm seven times went the black leather straps that secured the phylactery against the crisp, starched cotton of his white business shirt. Once he had wound the straps seven times, he tightened them in one fluid motion.

The box was angled so that it faced in the direction of his heart. His movements were swift and sure, free of the tentativeness and sorrow I sensed in him during the rest of his waking hours. As he began his morning prayers, he came into focus: he seemed to grow taller, more stately, as if in an artist's version of his finest self. I loved him best (and I remember him most clearly) as that swaying man, wrapped in his yellowed tallit, his voice rising and falling in waves.

I didn't know that worlds within worlds existed inside those small black boxes—any more than I was aware that invisible worlds existed within my father. Sealed inside the tefillin were parchment scrolls, on which four biblical passages—two from Exodus, two from Deuteronomy—were written in ink by a scribe. It would have taken the scribe many hours of unbroken concentration to complete the 3,188 minuscule Hebrew letters in four parallel columns, and if he had even a single nonreligious thought while writing, he would have to start all over again. (In the event that he had such a thought but did not confess, the entire apparatus would, I suppose, be tainted.) Once the ink had dried, the parchment would then have been bound with the thoroughly washed tail hair of a kosher animal, preferably a calf, and placed inside the leather boxes, which were made from the skins of kosher live-stock as well.

Now—though he has been dead for over twenty years—I know my father much better than I did when he was alive. I have used all of my journalistic skills to dig into his history, and I have discovered that the man I watched each morning had already been through a lifetime of heartache: he had been betrayed by his first wife, then divorced; his beloved second wife died six months after their wedding; his marriage to his third wife, my mother, was contentious and disappointing; he was depressed, and suffered from chronic pain; he obsessed about his own physical health, and lived in terror of sudden death; he took tranquilizers by the handful. So what was his relationship to his morning prayers? Did he enact this ritual because it gave him some small measure of comfort? Or simply because it was habit? Did he think God was listening? And if God was listening now, where had he disappeared to during all the trouble?

In a chaotic world—a world that had failed my father—at least here in the quiet den of his suburban home, he knew what was required of him. He made quick work of his morning prayers. The ritual seemed to enliven him; it gave him a sense of his purpose and place. By laying tefillin—*and you shalt bind them as a sign upon your hand, and they shall be for frontlets between your eyes*—he was fulfilling one of many daily obligations; wearing them meant that he remembered that God brought the children of Israel out of Egypt.

The daily business of being an observant Jew was pretty much a full-time job: *And you shall speak of them when you sit at home, and when* you walk along the way, and when you lie down and when you rise up. We were supposed to be in an unending state of gratitude to God for all he had done for us. Otherwise, it went without saying, God might get seriously pissed off. This is why we had a mezuzah affixed to each doorpost of our entire house except the closets and bathrooms, with another parchment scroll inside, containing further words from Deuteronomy: *And thou shalt write them upon the doorposts of thy house and upon thy gates.* This was why we had two sinks and two dishwashers in our kitchen, to keep dairy and meat separate. *Thou shalt not seethe a kid in its mother's milk.* And this was why my parents slept in twin beds—so that for seven days after the onset of my mother's period, she wouldn't contaminate my father with her impurity. There was a blessing or a prayer for everything, lest we forget, even for a moment, that our purpose in life was to appease and serve a very moody God.

After he had completed his morning prayers, my father unraveled the leather straps, wound them back into tight coils, and placed them, along with his tallit, back in the blue velvet pouch. Then he took off his yarmulke, put on his suit jacket, and took the train to Wall Street. He worked on the floor of the New York Stock Exchange, and he did not wear a yarmulke there. He wore the same tan jacket as all the other traders, crowded around the board to look at the rise and fall of the markets. He ate lunch at the Bull & Bear, rode the commuter train. Our family took trips, went on bike rides, ate dairy and fish in regular restaurants, played tennis. We did not wear the long dresses, the wigs, the black hats, the long beards or side curls that many of my cousins wear today. But still—thrumming beneath the surface, ever-present—there was the sense that my father's devotion was what allowed our world to keep turning. If he stopped—if he broke even one of the elaborate set of rules by which our family lived—something terrible might happen. After all, my father had to believe in a mercurial God who could be petitioned. Otherwise, he lived in a brutal and indifferent universe, governed by no entity, no greater being. When my father wore the tefillin, closed his eyes, and davened, he was doing what he could to protect himself and those he loved.

He who is accustomed to lay tefillin will live long, said Maimonides. *As it is written: "When the Lord is upon them, they will live."*

8.

Were there signs in the universe? And if so, when did they occur—and why? I had grown up fluent in the language of biblical metaphor: the snake in the garden, the parting of the Red Sea, the burning bush. And more recently, in adult life, the notion of signs had crept into many of my conversations with my friends: *I knew it was a sign that I should quit my job. I knew that it was a sign that something was wrong.* How was anybody supposed to know when something was a sign and when it was just a coincidence? Or maybe "signs" were merely a way of vesting coincidences with meaning.

I had never thought of God as a micromanager. I didn't think he was up there sending secret signals to me and the nearly seven billion other people who inhabit the planet. As far as I knew, he had never gotten me a parking space. And so, to the degree that

I gave credence to signs at all, I didn't think they were coming from God—at least not in that man-with-a-white-beard-in-the-sky kind of way. So then, what were these signs—if indeed, they existed? A person could make herself crazy with this.

The weather report is a sign that I shouldn't drive into the city today.

Running into that editor is a sign that I should write for her magazine.

That twinge in my side is a sign that I should make a doctor's appointment.

As I continued to mull over these ideas, I also continued to peruse Kripalu's Web site, trying to convince myself to go on a meditation retreat. I did this in the same spirit in which I might read a complicated and time-consuming recipe for Black Forest cake. It was a nice, even *inspired* idea, but when it came to actually doing it . . . well, it probably wasn't going to happen. It was too foreign, too daunting.

One afternoon, during this time, a friend took me to a yoga class. It was a strenuous class, and by the time we lay on our backs in final relaxation, I was in a highly receptive state. Final relaxation—the Sanskrit word is *shavasana*, or corpse pose—is considered by many to be the most important pose in yoga. In *shavasana*—lying still, arms and legs spread slightly apart, breath relaxed, palms facing upward, eyes closed—everything slows down. The physical body is restored, the mind released. I have often experienced a freedom from my usually racing thoughts in *shavasana*, as well as a kind of openness. A vulnerability to *what is*.

As we all lay quietly on our mats, the teacher read a passage from a poem. *Inside and outside her head, a billion, trillion stars, beyond count, circled and exploded . . . Songs were heard in spheres within spheres, electric, crackle, sharp. She heard nothing. How could she, when not once had she even heard the sound of her own breathing?*

The words entered my consciousness like a simple, pure strain of music. It seemed to me that, like the woman in the poem, I wasn't hearing my own breath. I was always either stuck in the past, or obsessing about the future, while the present heaped its gifts on me, screaming for attention. I wrote down the name of the poet, Duane Michaels, and as soon as I got home, I looked him up on the Internet, along with *the sound of her own breathing*. I needed to get my hands on that poem. I scrolled through the search results and stopped at a reference to a book, *Yoga and the Quest for the True Self* by a writer named Stephen Cope. Who was this Stephen Cope? I had never heard of him. And besides, I owned too many yoga books that I hadn't read. Still, on a whim—there were more sensible, not to mention less expensive, ways to find the poem—I bought his book.

When the book arrived, something about it seemed to call out to me. Unlike the many books that I ordered from Amazon.com, which were driven up our hill by the UPS truck and left in boxes on our porch, I started to read this one as soon as I pulled it from its wrapping. How can I explain this? It was as if the receptive state of *shavasana* had propelled me to take one small action. Then another. And another. I had stepped into a stream and was now being carried along by an unfamiliar, powerful current. The book was ostensibly about yoga metaphysics. A deadly subject—worthy of a spot at the far bottom of my pile—but instead, I couldn't stop turning the pages. A page-turner of yoga metaphysics! I carried it with me everywhere, savoring it; I underlined whole passages, scribbled asterisks and exclamation points in the margins.

I brought the book with me, one early evening, as I drove an hour to a fund-raiser for a library in the northern part of my county. I had agreed to participate in this literary event, even though it was the kind of thing I often declined. The air was hot and muggy, and as a crowd began to gather beneath a big tent, I regretted having agreed to come. I made a mental note to be more careful with my time in the future. One of the library volunteers led me over to a table where my books were piled in front of me. I knew these events; guests at the fund-raiser would pick up my books, weigh them in their hands, ask me if they were good reads. Then they would cross the grass to the other side of the tent and buy a best-selling cookbook instead.

I fanned myself with my program as the other author sharing the table with me took a seat. He was an elegant man with a kind, chiseled face. He had bright blue eyes, which he fixed on me with a smile. He reached over to shake my hand.

"Hi, Steve Cope," he said.

Turn right, turn left. Stay home that day. Take a different route. Cross the street for no apparent reason. Say yes, say no. Get up from the breakfast table, slip into the elevator just as the doors are closing. Book the afternoon flight. Drive exactly sixty-three miles per hour. Flip a coin. Call it coincidence, luck, fate, destiny, randomness. Some would call it the hand of God. I wasn't sure what to call it. What I did know is that this was a huge, blinking neon sign I couldn't ignore or dismiss. All these seemingly disconnected bits—a new yoga class, a teacher's particular selection of a poem, the wonders of Google and Amazon, an impulsive one-click purchase, an agreement to participate in a local charity event—all these formed a pattern, invisible to see. *Do this*, a gentle voice seemed to be saying. *Now this. And now this.* All of which had led me to be seated next to Stephen Cope: author, yogi, scholar—and director of the Institute for Extraordinary Living at Kripalu.

9.

On our last afternoon in Venice, Michael, Jacob, and I arrived at the Jewish ghetto just as the synagogue was closing. We had spent a few days in that magical city wandering around more typical tourist sights: San Marco, the Rialto Bridge, the Peggy Guggenheim Museum. I hadn't really wanted to go to the ghetto—and in the past I would have left it off our itinerary. For years, I had avoided the Jewish stuff. Hadn't I already had enough of it? But deep down, beneath layers of discomfort, there was something I wanted to know. Some powerful piece of my identity, withered like an underused muscle.

It was a raw day in March, and by the time we took the vaporetto all the way down the Grand Canal and wound our way through the narrow streets to the ghetto, it had become dark and cold.

One shop was open, though. The Judaica store. Silver menorahs gleamed in the brightly lit windows. Intricate mezuzahs were lined up on jewel-colored velvet.

"Let's buy a mezuzah," I said to Michael. I had come here with no such intention, but now it seemed like the thing to do. We had dozens of mezuzahs in our basement, from every home my parents had lived in, but I had never once considered digging one up and affixing it to the doorpost of our house.

We wandered into the store. An elderly woman was in back, behind the cash register. She looked like she owned the place, which we later found out she did. Her husband was the master silversmith who crafted all of the Judaica: pointers, crowns, breastplates—everything needed to dress the Torah. As she glanced up at us, I was aware of what we looked like, as a family. With my long blond hair, I must be the shiksa wife of a Jewish man, and here was our little blond son. I had an irrational desire to announce my Jewishness. *Raised Orthodox! Grew up kosher! Two sinks, two refrigerators—no kidding!*

Michael and I began examining various mezuzahs. There were big ones and small ones, modern-looking ones, and others designed with the delicate Venetian silver openwork I had seen in shops around the city.

"What is this?" Jacob asked, turning one over.

My breath caught at the fact that my son did not recognize a mezuzah. But of course he didn't. Why would he?

"That's a mezuzah," I answered. "We're supposed to put it on the doorpost of our house."

"Why?"

"Because we're Jewish."

It was a lame answer, but the best I could do at the time.

"How about this one?" Michael handed me a lovely small mezuzah. I tried to picture it attached to the frame of our kitchen door. We have a stone porch, piled with wood. A bench, on which ski equipment collects during winter, baseball bats and gloves during summer. And suddenly I felt exhausted, completely overwhelmed. I stood in the store, weighing the mezuzah in my hand. I wanted to leave immediately.

"Maybe we should just forget it," I said to Michael. "I don't know. It's kind of silly—I mean, we have all those mezuzahs in the basement."

"No, let's do this. It's beautiful—and special that we're buying it here. Together."

I knew Michael didn't care about the actual mezuzah. But he was having a rare sentimental moment, and Jacob was curious—so what was my problem? As the woman wrapped it up carefully, packing it into a special box for our journey home, I felt paralyzed. How could we buy only one? We needed to buy—here I started counting all the doorways of our house—at least fourteen. If we were going the mezuzah route, then we needed to put one on each and every doorway except for closets and bathrooms. And who would affix it to the doorpost? Did it need a special blessing? Where would I find a rabbi? Which side did it go on, anyway? This was the way it had always been for me: all or nothing, I realized, invariably led to nothing.

"Let's go." I tugged at Michael's sleeve.

But he had already given the woman his credit card, and as we stepped out onto the wet cobblestone streets of the ghetto, we carried with us a plastic bag containing a single, beautiful mezuzah.

10.

These days, when I am in the middle of my yoga practice—and if I allow it to happen—my jaw will begin to shake violently. My teeth will chatter. My throat will open up, becoming almost hollow, as if a scream is trying to escape. In the midst of my peaceful, contented life, a wave crashes over me. As I lie on the floor, folded into child's pose, I try to stay with the physical sensation. It's hard, scary, completely out-of-control. Still, I try to let it come—to welcome it, even. I know it has lessons to teach me. But what if it doesn't stop? What if the shaking and chattering go on and on, and I turn into one of those people you see on the street, talking to herself? There are stories inside of me, hardened into tight little knots. Call them anything: Sanskrit *samskaras*, disturbances in the field, sediment scraped from the depths. They are at the core of all the other stories that are easier to tell. *My father died sad. My mother died angry. The family of my childhood has become dust.*

II.

"We have an answer, and it isn't the one we had hoped for," the doctor said. In his cramped office, he had moved his chair around to the other side of his desk, so he could sit close to Michael and me. I registered that this wasn't a good sign.

He laid out a long printout of an EEG on his desk, flattened it, then traced the jagged lines of its peaks and valleys with one finger, as if pointing out directions on a map. I leaned forward and studied it, like I might be able to understand. My six-month-old baby was asleep in my arms. He had cried himself to sleep during the EEG, salty rivers of tears dried on his soft cheeks. His hair—those blond curls—was matted down and smelled of the chemical goop the technician had used to attach the electrodes.

As the doctor spoke, I scribbled down words in a notebook previously used for shopping lists. *Hypsarrhythmia, West syndrome, infantile spasms, seizure disorder. Very rare, seven out of a million babies.* I wrote down everything he said, because the words were coming too fast, a torrent. They were disintegrating, falling apart in my mind. I kept looking down at my perfect, beautiful Jacob. His tear-streaked cheek, his shell of an ear.

"We have to work on stopping the seizures immediately," the doctor said. "There are a limited number of medications we can try—the most effective one isn't FDA approved. But we can help you to get it from a pharmacy in Canada, or Mexico—"

"What happens?" Michael's voice sounded like it was coming from a cave. "What happens if the seizures aren't stopped?"

"Brain damage," said the doctor. He didn't blink, or hesitate. He said it softly. On his bookshelf, I noticed, there was a photograph of him with his wife and daughter, at what appeared to be his daughter's college graduation.

The bones in Michael's face seemed to shift. I reached over and held his hand, held it tight. What was going to happen to us?

"Every minute counts," the doctor said. "Every seizure has an effect."

The doctor's receptionist knocked on his office door.

"I reached the Kramers," she said to the doctor.

She handed us a page from a prescription pad, with an address scribbled on it.

"This family has a child who is taking the medication you need. I've called them—they're expecting you. They'll lend you some."

We drove crosstown in our safe and solid Volvo, with Jacob strapped into his ergonomically designed, top-of-the-line infant car seat. He was dressed in his organic cotton T-shirt and baby jeans, which had been washed in natural laundry soap. We pulled up in front of a high-rise on West Ninety-sixth Street. I had passed the building a hundred times or more in the years I had lived in the city. In what seemed another life, I had speed-walked down Ninety-sixth Street on my way to the Central Park reservoir. I had dined at a nearby restaurant during a bad blind date. Now, I waited in the back of the car with my sleeping baby as my husband rode the elevator up to apartment 28F, where a stranger was waiting to give him a packet of medication—our only hope of saving our son's life.

12.

I didn't believe that God had caused this to happen. Nor did I believe that, by praying to him, he would spare us. Still, every moment of every day became a prayer. The medication came in the form of a powder, delivered via FedEx from a pharmacy in Toronto. Each packet of powder—which was fine and white— had to be divided into five even doses. The ritual of chopping the powder with a razor blade into perfect lines became a prayer.

I searched for reasons—a way of understanding being on the

wrong side of such a statistic. *Seven out of a million babies.* Somebody had to be one of the seven, didn't they? Why us? Why *not* us? I blamed the environment: maybe it was the pesticide we had used to get rid of the yellow-jacket nest outside Jacob's window. I blamed modern medicine: maybe it was the DPT vaccination he had received at his six-month checkup. But mostly, I blamed myself. I was the mother. It had to be my fault, somehow. Maybe it was the raw tuna I ate before I knew I was pregnant. Or the stress of my last book tour. If I were a devout Jew, there would be a blessing and a petitioning: *Blessed art Thou, O Lord, our God, King of the Universe, the True Judge.* If I were a practicing Christian: *Thy will be done, on Earth as it is in Heaven.*

Never once did it occur to me to blame God—nor to ask him for any special favors. Yet my prayers continued. Watching my baby's face for signs of his eyes flickering upward, his hands and legs making involuntary motions, I held my breath as if my breath itself were a prayer. Each night, I rocked Jacob to sleep— as I had since the day he was born—and I sang him a lullaby. Now that lullaby was as long and meditative and devotional as the Amidah. I sang "Hush, Little Baby" three times. If I missed even a single word, I had to start all over again. Next—even if he was fast asleep—came two rounds of "Twinkle, Twinkle, Little Star." Then I closed my eyes until all was darkness. I counted backward from fifty in silence. *Please watch over my baby and keep him safe. Please keep him safe,* I whispered over and over again. *Please.* Never once did I wonder who—if anyone—might be listening.

13.

I sat on a meditation cushion near the back of a vast semicircle of meditation cushions, as close to the door as possible. A couple of hundred people filled the great hall: old, young, thin, fat, in torn sweatshirts and trendy velour. Lots of tattoos—mandalas, oms, colorful birds, indecipherable Sanskrit words inscribed on biceps, ankles, sacrums. Bare feet with overgrown, yellowed toenails, or perfect bright pink pedicures. Most of the crowd looked like they had been to Kripalu—or to places like Kripalu—many times before. I could spot the regulars, the ones who were familiar with the floor plans of Esalen and Spirit Rock, for whom *retreat* was more a noun than a verb. They were settled in, comfortable; water bottles by their sides, special pens and pads for taking notes.

And what about me? *Breathe.* I felt like I had taken a wrong turn, gotten off at the wrong exit. I should have been at the Canyon Ranch resort down the road, getting a hot stone massage. I needed to relax—and spa treatments seemed a lot more relaxing than sitting erect on a meditation cushion with hundreds of strangers. But I wasn't here to relax—at least not in that way. I needed some space in my head. I was practically hyperventilating, taking in sips of air as I waited for the morning program to start. Instead of the world opening up to me, it had grown increasingly constricted. The walls closing in.

The morning program was about to begin. Two upholstered chairs were set up at the front of the great hall, a table with two glasses and a bottle of water between them. An easel stood next to the chairs, supporting a large dry-erase board, upon which a list was written.

Metta: Lovingkindness
Maitri: Friendliness
Karuna: Compassion
Mudita: Sympathetic joy
Upekkha: Equanimity

I studied the list. Couldn't argue with any of that, really. I needed greater doses of all of the above, but perhaps equanimity most of all. It seemed, after eleven years of marriage, that I had forgotten how to be on my own. I watched as Steve Cope—the only reason I had made this trip—approached the front of the great hall and settled into one of the chairs, then crossed his legs in lotus position. He was joined by his co-leader of this three-day workshop, Sylvia Boorstein, a well-respected Buddhist teacher whose books, with titles like *Don't Just Do Something, Sit There* and *It's Easier Than You Think*, were featured downstairs in the Kripalu bookstore.

Sylvia began by slowly gazing around the entire semicircle. She seemed to make eye contact with every single person in the room. She was a diminutive woman, perhaps in her early seventies, with short gray hair and an impish, dare I say Buddha-like, face.

"The whole world is a lesson in what's true," she said. "Everyone is struggling. Life is difficult for everybody. Once you're in, there's no way out. You have to go forward. And we all die in the end. So how to deal with it?"

The words sliced through everything: through my racing mind, my rapid pulse, my general state of agitation. That was it, wasn't it? In a few simple sentences she had addressed the essence of what I felt. She knew about the roller coaster, the slow ascent, the rapid downward plunge. I was here. I had reached my life. I had built it by decision and by accident—and there would be no other. *So how to deal with it?* I fixed all of my attention on Sylvia Boorstein. I had come to Kripalu because of Steve Cope, but here was a surprise in the form of this little Jewish grandmother. If she could articulate the questions so succinctly, maybe she had some answers.

"*Metta* meditation," she went on, "is a concentration practice. It's the protection formula that the Buddha taught the monks: one of being able to depend on your own good heart. So"—she clasped her hands together—"how do we do this? By tempering one's own heart and restoring it to balance. *Metta* is a practice of inclining the mind in the direction of good will."

Sylvia then laid out for us her four favorite phrases—variations on the Buddha's original phrases—to chant silently during *metta*:

> *May I feel protected and safe.*
> *May I feel contented and pleased.*
> *May my physical body support me with strength.*
> *May my life unfold smoothly with ease.*

The idea was to silently repeat the phrases again and again, at first focusing on ourselves, but then eventually directing the phrases to others: our closest teachers and benefactors; then our loved ones; our friends; strangers; and eventually—after much practice—to those with whom we have difficult relationships, or as it is known in Buddhist scripture, our enemies.

Sylvia paused, glancing at the large clock hanging on the back wall, behind us. "Let's sit for a few minutes."

I closed my eyes. A few minutes. What was Sylvia Boorstein's idea of a few minutes? But despite the difficulty of sitting still, I felt myself slowing down. The phrases gave my overactive mind a place to settle, a single point of concentration, a word at a time. When I felt myself becoming distracted, I pulled myself back to the repetition. Faces drifted pleasantly through my head: an old college professor, my mother-in-law, my father-in-law, Michael, Jacob, a succession of friends. As soon as I finished one round of phrases, another person seemed to rise into my consciousness, as if waiting on line. But after a little while, I became troubled by the question of prayer. Was this a prayer? Who was it directed to? Was I petitioning some almighty being? The God of my childhood asserted himself: judging, withholding, all-knowing. In turn, the phrases themselves became supplication, bargaining, appeasement. My mind was aswirl once again, and I could barely sit still. I wondered if it was okay to get up to go to the bathroom, or whether I'd disturb everyone and become the retreat pariah.

Just when I thought I couldn't handle another second, Sylvia sounded a gong, and people opened their eyes, stretched out. I looked around from my meditation cushion. Many appeared beatific, even glowing. A middle-aged woman a few rows in front of me, with a wild mass of salt-and-pepper hair and a leather ankle bracelet, was smiling as tears poured down her cheeks.

"What did you all experience?" Sylvia asked after a long pause.

Her voice was so familiar to me: lilting, slightly hoarse, street-smart, and kind. A raised-in-Brooklyn-by-Yiddish-speaking-immigrant-parents voice. She reminded me of my mentor, the writer Grace Paley, who had recently died. No one had ever reminded me of Grace before.

I raised my hand. This was so unlike me that I looked up at my own hand as if it belonged to someone else. But I really did have a question. It had been bubbling up inside me and was banging against my rib cage, my pounding heart, demanding an answer.

"Yes." Sylvia pointed. A cordless microphone was passed to me.

"I was raised in a very religious home," I began, sounding shaky. "And I'm confused about God. So I found it hard—I mean . . . to whom are we speaking?"

Sylvia tilted her head to the side. A smile played at her lips, as if she had been expecting this question, and was delighted by it.

"I don't think it has to be metaphysical," she said. "It's the expression of a *wish*, really."

A wish. After the morning session ended, I wandered the halls of Kripalu, lost in thought. I barely registered the lunchtime crowd of people carrying colorful trays piled high with bowls of salad and grains. Wishing was something children did—wasn't it? I pictured Jacob's face as he stood in front of a fountain, clutching a penny (though of course nickels or quarters were far better) in his fist. Or the way, on the banks of the Shepaug River, he had tossed his bread during *tashlich*, his expression serious, concentrated, intent.

As an adult, I had long since given up on wishing. It seemed the equivalent of sprinkling magic fairy dust. But really, what did it mean to fervently, wholeheartedly name a desire? *May you feel pro-tected and safe.* To speak out of a deep yearning—to set that yearn-ing loose in the world? *May you feel contented and pleased.* Could a wish be a less fraught word for a prayer? *May your physical body support you with strength.* Maybe it wasn't about who, if anyone, was on the other end, listening. Maybe faith had to do with holding up one end of the dialogue. *May your life unfold smoothly, with ease.*

14.

The eleven benefits of *metta* according to the Buddha:
    People who practice *metta* . . .
    Sleep peacefully
    Wake peacefully
    Dream peaceful dreams
    People love them
    Angels love them
    Angels will protect them
    Poisons and weapons and fire won't harm them
    Their faces are clear
    Their minds are serene
    They die unconfused
    And live in heavenly realms.

15.

When Sylvia gave us the list of *metta's* benefits, she asked us to think about which one most resonated with us personally. Then, following a long meditation, she asked for a show of hands for each benefit.

Sleep peacefully was definitely a favorite.

People love them was pretty popular too.

And certainly *poisons and weapons and fire won't harm them* had its fans. But there was one benefit that stood out for me as if it were electric. It seemed to hold within it the key to all the others. I was the only person in that vast room to raise her hand for *to die unconfused.*

16.

"I never forgave your mother for marrying your father."

My mother's oldest friend was tipsy, and this was her opening gambit. The ice in her plastic cup of vodka rattled. I had come to this art gallery in upstate New York precisely to see the friend. My mother had been dead for a few years, and I was on a mission— doing detective work, after the fact. I had spent my childhood and the better part of my early adulthood trying to understand my mother. She had been an extraordinarily difficult person, spiteful and full of rage, with a temper that could flare, seemingly out of nowhere, scorching everything and everyone who got in its way. Who had my mother been? I kept hoping that someone who knew her well—or at least better than I did—would be able to fill in some missing pieces to the puzzle: why had she been so bitterly angry, so disappointed, so . . . lost? As she was dying, she had turned to me in a state of great, almost childlike puzzlement: "But I was just getting my life together," she said. How was it possible, after nearly eighty years on the planet, that she had felt she was just getting her life together? Maybe if I could see her more clearly—even after death—she would lose some of her power to haunt me. Sometimes, at home in Connecticut, I would spot a huge black crow pecking at the tall grass in our front meadow. Not that I believed in signs, or anything. But nonetheless: *There she is*, I would think. *There's Irene.*

"She was brilliant, your mother," said the friend. "*Brilliant*"— she underscored her point. "And she was an atheist. What was an atheist doing marrying an Orthodox Jew—with two sinks and two dishwashers?"

I became very still, sensing danger. *Brilliant* and *atheist* were two words I had never associated with my mother. A memory materialized: it was the year before my bat mitzvah. She was standing next to me at Temple Shomrei Torah, on a rare Saturday morning when she accompanied my father and me to shul. It was the end of the Shabbos service, and she confidently sang "Adon Olam" with the rest of the congregation, even though she didn't know the words.

My mother's friend leaned toward me. She seemed intent on getting to the bottom of this. "Why would your mother have become religious like that?" She was slurring her words slightly.

She was eighty years old; the vodka had gone to her head. "The holidays, the cooking, the endless rules? What could she have been thinking?"

But I had stopped listening. A bit of my childhood had been snipped loose and now I was hearing it loud and clear. I was no longer in the art gallery, but back in Hillside, New Jersey. Back between my parents.

Adon Olam, asher melach, b'terem kol, y'tzir nivro . . .

My mother sat on one side of me, my father on the other. This—men and women sitting together in a Conservative shul—was not how my father preferred to daven. We used to belong to an Orthodox shul, where men and women were separated by a *mechitzah*, so that the men wouldn't be distracted during their prayers. But my mother had gotten into a huge fight with Rabbi Teitz, and we had never been back.

My father sang loudly in his Ashkenazic Hebrew. I leaned in his direction, trying to distance myself from my mother. The stained-glass windows of Shomrei Torah were new, jewel-colored, casting rainbows of light on the pale wood of the pews, the bimah where Rabbi Lasker stood in his white robe. Outside the nondescript one-story synagogue, Saturday-morning traffic whizzed by on Union Avenue.

V'im ruchi, g'viyati, Adonai li v'loa ira Adon Olam.

Prayer books snapped closed, the morning service finally over. Did I think about the meaning of what I was singing? *And with my soul, my body too, God is with me, I shall not fear*, set to a very cheerful little tune.

"Good Shabbos." My father's Sabbath stubble was rough against my cheek.

"Good Shabbos." My mother kissed my forehead.

We walked home single file, using the shortcut through the Pantirers' backyard, past their tennis court. As I stood in the upstate New York art gallery—my father twenty years gone, my mother four—I could taste the Shabbos lunch my mother had waiting for us at home: cold sliced brisket and peas, a day-old challah from the kosher bakery. Lunch was the same every Saturday: she pulled the brisket, wrapped in Saran, from the refrigerator, spooned thawed peas into a china bowl. She placed the challah on its special silver and wood plate, along with a serrated silver knife. The challah was covered by a silk cloth embroidered with flowers and Hebrew lettering. Before we sat down to lunch, my father washed his hands, then made a quick blessing over the bread as he sliced it, crumbs flying in every direction. *Goddamnit, Paul!* My mother exploded. It happened like clockwork: the challah plate, the knife, the crumbs, my mother's rage. *Goddamnit!*

"She could have done anything, your mother," said the friend. "I used to ask her. I used to say, 'Irene, how can you live like this? Why would you live something you don't believe?'"

17.

"Did you pray when Jacob was sick?" I asked Michael, years later.

We were in our bright, sunny kitchen. Through the window—beyond the stone patio and herb garden—I could see Jacob in the backyard. He was throwing himself fly balls, making diving catches with his outstretched mitt, rolling on the grass. Picturing himself at Fenway Park.

Michael looked at me as if I had asked him if he practiced voodoo, or burned incense at an altar. "Um—no. It never occurred to me. Did you?"

My rocking chair ritual, my incessant pleading—it had been silent, private. I never said a word about it to Michael. What else was there to do? Beyond the MRIs, the CT scans, the second opinions, the research on the Internet, the national experts—what else was there to do but say *please?*

"Yes," I said. "I prayed."

"Did it help?"

The question stopped me. *Did it help.* The fact is, I couldn't *not* pray. I didn't break it down, or intellectualize it. I suppose it made me feel like I was doing everything I possibly could. That's what my obsessive jumble of lullabies and counting backward was all about. It didn't cross my mind to call a rabbi, or to seek spiritual guidance of any kind. *Please save my child.* In the unlikely event that anyone was listening, I wanted to be sure to be heard. I was taking no chances—the same way that I cupped my hands on top of Jacob's head and willed the firestorm inside his brain to subside.

"It certainly didn't hurt," I said.

18.

When I was growing up in New Jersey, I had a crush on a family— the entire family—who lived in our neighborhood: Arnold, Shirley, Harvey, Eddie, and Joyce Adler. The Adlers were like gods to me. Every spare moment, when I wasn't playing field hockey or practicing piano or doing homework, I got on my bike and rode circles around their house, hoping someone would notice and invite me in. The kids were a lot older than I was. The year I was fifteen, Harvey graduated from medical school in New York. Eddie was in medical school in Philadelphia. And Joyce was a freshman at the University of Vermont.

The Adlers were beautiful and bright and happy. Their home always seemed lit from within, not only by glowing lamps and a steady hum of activity, but by something I couldn't have put my finger on at the time. To me, they seemed *blessed*. Life in the Adler household was in sharp contrast to the tension and loneliness I felt with my own parents—but that wasn't it. The reason for my infatuation with that family was their certainty, their absolute conviction that they lived in a world designed to please and reward them. They would always have whatever they wanted. Life would continue as planned: they were charmed, gifted, golden, and admission to their inner circle meant that some of that charm might rub off on me.

Each winter, the family spent their Christmas vacation on the Caribbean island of Antigua. They stayed at the same hotel, played tennis with the same pro, ordered the same frozen drinks on the beach. Once, I asked them if they were planning to go to Antigua that year. The oldest son, Harvey, answered this way: *Does the sun rise in the east and set in the west?*

This might, in retrospect, appear to be hubris, but really it was a form of innocence. Nothing bad had ever happened to any of the Adlers. It was an elegant, if flawed, bit of logic to proceed from there to the certitude that nothing ever would.

But then, after their annual Caribbean holiday—from which they returned tanned and languid—Joyce went back to college and suffered a massive stroke, from which she never recovered. In the blink of an eye, she became paralyzed and mute, trapped inside her own body. It was an inexplicable, freak occurrence. She spent the rest of her life—I recently heard that she passed away in her forties—living at home with her parents. Wheelchair ramps replaced outdoor steps. The basket of sports equipment next to the garage doors disappeared forever. The family closed ranks. For the rest of my teenage years, I continued to circle the house on my bicycle whenever I could, but never again was I invited inside.

It has been many years since I've heard word of the Adlers. My parents moved away from the New Jersey suburb where we all lived. But their story is embedded somewhere within me, a *samskara*. Had they been foolish to believe in their own good fortune for all that time—to trust that all would be well? They weren't religious people, but they had a kind of blind faith. I, on the other hand, come from a long line of religious people who aren't so sure that the sun will rise in the east and set in the west—much less that their own lives will unfold predictably. I was born and bred to fear the worst. And I know that the worst either happens or it doesn't. Worry is not a form of protection. So who's the fool?

Occasionally I search for the Adlers on the Internet. Not much information is available. The sons have both become ophthalmologists, like their father. They've established private practices; moved to more affluent suburbs; had a few kids. I find myself wondering how those kids—heirs to the family whose innocence was so suddenly and completely crushed—have been raised to think of themselves. What have they inherited from the past? Do they feel blessed? Certain of their own specialness? Do they make assumptions about the future? Or perhaps they live in fear of the other shoe dropping. After all, it dropped once.

19.

I was watching Jacob build a tower of alphabet blocks when the first plane hit.

Six, seven, eight, nine . . . I had been busy trying to remember how many blocks a two-and-a-half-year-old was supposed to be able to stack. And I was mentally ticking off the checklist from *What to Expect: The Toddler Years.* I did this all the time. I kept a well-worn paperback edition by my bedside. It was like my Bible. Each night I read about developmental milestones he should have/might have/could even possibly have reached.

As I watched him play, I registered the sound of a tremendous but distant boom. Something had happened somewhere nearby, but not too nearby. A truck accident on Flatbush Avenue, maybe. A tractor trailer slamming across one of those uneven metal plates. We lived in brownstone Brooklyn, in a red brick Federal town house we had bought and moved into right after Jacob was born. It was in a neighborhood "in transition," as the real estate brokers liked to say, which was why we had been able to afford a four-story house there. From our roof, we could see the towers of the World Trade Center.

Ten, eleven, twelve . . .

I had been sticking very close to home. My life had become

small, concentrated, a single, pinpoint beam of light focused on my son. I didn't like being far away from Jacob. Distance made me nervous. To go from our house into Manhattan meant a subway ride over a bridge, or under the East River. Each time I squeezed myself through the doors of a crowded train, my heart felt like it was going to explode—a flood building, my veins expanding as the train pulled away from the platform. And so I stayed nearby—writing in my study upstairs, or at a Starbucks in Park Slope. I told myself I liked it this way. It wasn't because my baby had been so sick. It wasn't because we had medicated him around the clock for a year—waiting, watching for the tiniest flicker of his eyes, a sign of an infinitesimal seizure. No. Things were back to normal now—or so I told myself.

Jacob's babysitter arrived with the news that something—she wasn't sure what—had just happened. We turned on the television. It had been minutes since the first plane had hit, and the initial news coverage was chaos. One newscaster announced that this was a small, single-engine plane; another hypothesized that perhaps air traffic control had gone amok, steering the plane into the building.

"They're idiots." Michael shook his head. "Look at that fire. Only a commercial jet could do that."

Then the second jet banked and crashed.

We stood in our kitchen and stared at the screen.

"Terrorism," Michael said.

I had never seen him like this. His eyes were blinking rapidly, but he was preternaturally calm. I could practically see his mind running through the possibilities. In his life before I knew him,

Michael had been a war correspondent. This kind of composure had saved his life a dozen times.

"Are we in danger here?"

My mind raced. What to do? Where to go?

I held Jacob, keeping his face turned away from the images on the TV. He squirmed in my arms as I moved through the house. I couldn't stand still. I paced from room to room, looking around wildly. The antique chandelier hanging in the foyer, the polished wood shutters in the parlor—I had been under the illusion that my family's home was safe and solid. I caught a glimpse of Jacob and me in the mirror above the fireplace. We were a blur. We could become rubble at any second.

"Mommy, *down!*"

Jacob scrambled up the steep stairs to his bedroom. For once, I didn't stop to mentally consult *What to Expect* about whether he should have used a full sentence. *What to Expect* was suddenly, ludicrously irrelevant. He sat on the organic cotton carpet and went back to work, stacking blocks again.

The first tower collapsed. A dark, acrid cloud.

The phone rang. A friend whose husband worked at the *Wall Street Journal*—he had left for work that morning and now she couldn't find him.

It rang again.

"Do you have a bike?"

Now it was Jacki Lyden, our friend and neighbor, and an NPR correspondent.

"What?"

"A bicycle, Dani—do you have a bike?"

Within minutes, she appeared breathless at our door and grabbed the rickety bicycle we kept in the basement. I still didn't get it. I thought Jacki would be riding far away—maybe all the way up to the tip of Long Island, where she would then charter a boat to a safer place. I didn't understand that some people would actually choose to *go toward the disaster*. That if Michael weren't married to me and the father of our little boy, he, too, would have gone in that direction. I later found out that we had several friends—journalists, all of them—who rushed to lower Manhattan that day. As the dust-covered, devastated throngs of thousands crossed the Brooklyn Bridge, heading away from the hole ripped through the heart of the city, there were those who headed straight for it.

20.

I went to see the osteopath in his Connecticut office on the ground floor of a house at the end of a quiet village street. The whole way there, I kept wanting to turn the car around. What was I doing? Where was I going—and why? A poet friend had recommended this guy. I had told her about how I had been grinding my teeth in my sleep. About how, during my yoga practice, my jaw would sometimes start to tremble, trying to release. I was surprised when she suggested an osteopath. Weren't they bone doctors for old people? But I was willing to give him a try; the poet friend told me that he had changed her life. It seemed to me that anyone who has changed someone's life is worth meeting.

"Any history of injuries?" he began our session.

I shook my head.

"None? No bad falls—not even in childhood?"

I searched my memory. "No," I answered.

He looked surprised, but it was true: I had never really fallen. He swiveled on his chair and made a notation on my brand-new chart. His office didn't look like a typical doctor's office. No equipment, not even a scale. Scattered on his desk were a blood pressure cuff, a stethoscope, and a half-empty glass of water.

"Surgery? Hospitalizations?"

"Other than giving birth—no."

"Cancer, diabetes, high blood pressure, cardiovascular problems?"

No, no, and no. I felt a potent combination of lucky and fearful.

The doctor probed more deeply into my family history. It is one of the guiding principles of osteopathy to treat the whole patient. I had learned this in the last fifteen minutes, by thumbing through a well-worn paperback about osteopathy in the waiting room: *Dr. Fulford's Touch of Life: Aligning Body, Mind and Spirit to Honor the Healer Within.*

"What about your mother? Is she alive?"

"No. She died of lung cancer at eighty."

"And your father?"

"No—car accident," I answered. He winced slightly. I appreciated this. I watched his pen move across the page.

"At what age?"

"Sixty-four. Well, I should say"—here I faltered—"it's unclear why he died. He passed out behind the wheel of the car. He had been taking a lot of different prescription medications."

"Why?" The question came quickly, sharply.

"He'd had spinal surgery, and became addicted to the pain-killers."

The doctor nodded. He had seen a lot of this.

"What about your son? Any injuries?"

"A very rare seizure disorder when he was an infant," I said, and then rushed on before the doctor could wince again. "He's fine now."

My cheeks felt hot. I wanted the answers to my entire family history to be as simple and fortunate as my own good health. Parents still alive. Happy and thriving in their old age. A son with no medical history to speak of, beyond well-child pediatrician visits. Everything *just fine, thanks.* I knew that the jottings the doctor was making on his pad told a different story.

I lay faceup on a table as he placed his hands beneath me, gently applying a subtle, nearly undetectable pressure to my sacrum and spine. The office was dead quiet, except for the occasional chirp of a bird outside the window. Earlier, while I had been reading up on osteopathy in the waiting room, a woman—presumably a patient—had come in to make an appointment. She asked the receptionist if she had seen the deep purple flowers that had begun to bloom in that part of northern Connecticut. "I saw them in Massachusetts last week but hardly noticed," said the receptionist. "My relationship to them here is different."

I wasn't sure I would ever be someone contemplative enough to consider my relationship to flowers. I wasn't even sure I wanted to be. I secretly thought that this method of aligning of body, mind, and spirit—honor the healer within?—was probably a whole lot of hokum. But meanwhile, I was here. And through all the noise and clutter in my head, in such stark contrast to the silence surrounding me, I discovered that I was indeed experiencing something as the osteopath made his minuscule adjustments.

"What are you feeling right now?" he asked.

I kept my eyes closed.

"Sort of a flooding," I said. "A warmth in my head, my chest, my jaw."

"I would hope so."

"And a sense of well-being," I said. Puzzled. It was a well-being bordering on euphoria. Not my usual state. I gave in to it, floating. I felt soothed. I couldn't remember the last time I had felt so good.

At the end of the session—which might have lasted fifteen minutes or two hours—I sat up on the edge of the table. What had happened? The osteopath reached over to his bookcase and pulled out a heavy medical text. He then thumbed through it; there was something he wanted to show me. A detailed anatomical drawing of the spine and surrounding muscles and tissue.

"The chain ganglia"—he pointed to what looked like a strand of small beads—"are these nerves along the spinal cord right here. They're the part of the sympathetic nervous system responsible for delivering information about stress to the body—or, as it's more commonly known, the fight-or-flight response."

Fight or flight.

"Yours are out of whack," he said. "I can feel an inflammation."

No kidding.

"My chain ganglia," I repeated. From the depths of my euphoric state, I loved the sound of it: a gang, a chain gang gone crazy.

"It's hereditary," said the osteopath.

I thought about my father—the way he would sometimes be overcome by a sudden and inexplicable terror. His eyes would sharpen, and he would press two fingers against his carotid artery, checking his pulse. He carried with him a constant awareness of his own fragility. I had never understood how this fear coexisted alongside his faith. If he believed the religious doctrine by which he lived, wouldn't that have offered solace and protection? *And with my soul, my body too, God is with me, I shall not fear.* But here was a possible theory: my father's head and heart were in one place, but his chain ganglia were in another. Faith and fear—spirit and biochemistry in a constant tug-of-war.

And what about Jacob? He jumped at loud noises, covering his ears. He avoided scary movies, and had never been on a roller coaster. He wouldn't try any new food—not even if I bribed him. I hoped he had inherited Michael's cool, calm, collected genes— but I wouldn't bet on it.

"These nerves send your brain a signal that there's a tiger in the room," the doctor said. "Your neurons fire—your heart rate accelerates, your blood vessels constrict. Your whole body goes into survival mode. You think you're under attack, even when there's nothing there at all."

21.

After a few days—after the thin layer of ash blew away and the air no longer stung our eyes or burned our throats—I took Jacob out in his stroller. I wheeled him down the streets of Brooklyn along our usual route: across the wide, busy expanse of Flatbush and then down shady side streets lined with elegant brownstones to Seventh Avenue, the main commercial strip in Park Slope. We passed the Korean deli, the pizza place, the hardware store. The usual neighborhood types were out: an older man in a windbreaker scooped up his terrier's poop with a plastic baggie; a girl in a tank top drifted by, carrying a rolled-up yoga mat; a group of high school boys in falling-down pants congregated at the corner.

It seemed like a normal Park Slope morning, as long as you didn't look too closely. People were sitting on benches outside Ozzie's coffee shop, drinking their iced decaf lattes. Yoga classes had resumed. Strollers and dogs once again clogged the sidewalk. Shops were open, their signs—*25% off all silver jewelry! Brand-new shipment of Italian rustic table settings!*—like a relic of a sweet and innocent past life. But the faces of passersby told a different story: raw, dazed, going through the motions. We had been stripped down, as if a layer of skin had been removed. People met one another's eyes, nodded slightly. A recognition—Michael told me this happens in war zones—of a shared intimacy. We had been through something together, even if we never exchanged a word.

I didn't have any particular destination in mind as I wheeled

Jacob along. I wanted to be outside, to be around other people. Maybe to stop and get a frozen yogurt.

"And how are you, my little boo?" I asked Jacob, keeping up a constant one-way banter. "Everything all right down there?"

I saw the sign—*Warren Lewis Realty*—and stopped. I had walked past this real estate office dozens of times, had examined the pictures in its windows with Michael.

4 story single family Victorian. Mint, mint, mint!

North Slope 3 story. Needs TLC.

Michael and I kept an eye on brownstone prices. We had bought our house in Brooklyn at a good time, and had been enjoying watching the theoretical value of our house go up and up. For a couple of writers, it was as close as we had ever come to a windfall.

"We're going in here for a minute, okay?"

I wheeled Jacob through the doors of the office. Seated at a desk near the window, behind a computer monitor, was a man I recognized as one of the owners of the company. He looked up when I entered.

"Do you have time to talk?" I asked.

"Of course," he said. "Let's go sit outside."

He stood, then ushered me into the back. We passed rows of desks, most of them empty. A set of French doors led to a small, well-tended garden. I sat in a wrought-iron chair across a table from him.

"I think . . . ," I began. Took a deep breath and started again. "I think I might want to sell my house."

I hadn't planned on this—hadn't discussed it with Michael, even. Over the last few years, we had talked about living elsewhere. Seattle, Los Angeles, Marin County, Sag Harbor were a few places that had come up. But we had never been particularly serious. Just trying on different ways of living because . . . well, because we could. Jacob hadn't started school yet. Our family life hadn't taken root in one particular place, the way it would over the next few years. And we could do our work from anywhere—so why not?

But this was very different. I wanted *out*, I suddenly realized. And I wanted out *now*. I didn't want to move toward something as much as I wanted to move away from it. My awareness of this was immediate and stunning in its clarity.

"Let me give you one piece of advice," the real estate broker said. "You're the sixth person to walk in here today. Put your house on the market immediately. There's going to be a line behind you."

Birds chirped in the garden. In the distance, a siren. The metallic hiss of a city bus pulling into its stop. Urban sounds—as familiar to me as the cicadas and sprinkler systems of my own suburban childhood.

I looked down at Jacob, who had fallen asleep in his stroller. He was okay now. I had to remind myself of that every single day. He was healthy, seizure-free. Untouched by an illness that—like an enormous, nearly extinct bird—had soared across the landscape of our lives, casting its shadow over us before moving on.

"Let's do the paperwork," I said.

Tears rolled down the broker's cheeks. He made no attempt to wipe them away. He reached across the table—this stranger—and held my hand.

22.

My father's mother lived on the twenty-seventh floor of a huge prewar building on the corner of Seventy-second and Central Park West. The building—called the Majestic—was directly across from an entrance to the park. From high up in the tower, cyclists, roller skaters, dog walkers looked like colorful darting specks. The walking paths were dark gray ribbons, winding through swaths of green. The skyline of Fifth Avenue rose in the distance. But my grandmother wasn't able to see any of this. She had been bedridden, fading in and out of consciousness, for most of my childhood, since suffering a massive stroke at my grandfather's funeral.

My grandmother was cared for in her apartment by two nurse's aides who were with her all the time. Not a seat cushion was out of place in the formal living room. Ashtrays gleamed on coffee tables; inlaid marble floors were polished to a high gloss; crystal decanters sparkled in the bar, as if the whole apartment was prepared to wake up from a long and deep slumber. A portrait of my grandfather in a gilded frame hung above the fireplace mantel. Bald and imposing in a gray three-piece suit, he gazed sternly through his pince-nez, a green leather-bound volume of some sort held loosely in his hand. A Bible? Or perhaps a prop supplied by the artist to imply intellect—or piety.

Although visiting my grandmother used to frighten and unnerve me, still I looked forward to Sunday-morning drives into the city with my father when he went to see her. The city was my father's hometown. He had grown up there, and still retained traces of a New York accent. On our Sundays in New York he parked the car in a garage near his mother's apartment, and together we walked along the streets of the Upper West Side. Often, we stopped at Fine & Schapiro, a delicatessen on Seventy-second Street, where my father ordered his usual meal for us to share: turkey, tongue, coleslaw, and Russian dressing on rye, and a Dr. Brown's Cel-Ray soda. To this day, I can taste the sharp, carbonated celery, feel the sheer size of that sandwich as I tried to get my mouth around it to take a bite. I didn't understand that tongue was actually *tongue.*

A few blocks south of my grandmother's apartment, on a stretch of Broadway above Lincoln Center, stood an Orthodox shul that my grandfather had helped to create. When we passed that modern white building—as I did for many years into adulthood—I looked for my grandfather's name on the sign out front. *The Joseph Shapiro Institute.* I was proud to be a grandchild of this man I had never known, who had died when I was an infant. I treasured the single existing photograph of the two of us together: in the backyard of our house in Hillside, he sat on a chaise longue in his yarmulke and short-sleeved shirt, cradling me in his arms. As I grew up, I imagined he was watching me from a perch high up in the sky. He was that godlike to me. Being Joseph Shapiro's grandchild—the youngest of ten grandchildren—made me feel protected and special. It seemed we were enveloped in some kind of grace.

Years after I had fled the city that I loved—moving with my family to a part of Connecticut my grandparents would never have heard of—I was in town for a speaking engagement. A book club of employees at HBO had asked me to come talk to them during their lunch hour. That day, I was very much living in my mother's New York: I had stopped at Bergdorf Goodman to replace a lipstick. I wasn't conscious of it at the time, but when I wanted to feel close to my father, I did something Jewish. And when I wanted to feel close to my mother, I went shopping.

I walked out of the store on West Fifty-eighth Street and hailed a taxi. I gave the driver HBO's midtown address, then rummaged through my bag for my cell phone.

"You're lucky, you know—Fifth Avenue just opened up again. Traffic's been terrible."

Something about the voice: I felt it in my body before I registered anything else about it. The hard landing on the *k*. The soft, almost nonexistent *d*. A very specific accent—equal parts New York, New Jersey, and yeshiva. It was as if a piece of me had come loose. My eyes shot over to the identification card attached to the cloudy plastic partition. Then to the quadrant of the rearview mirror where his forehead was visible.

"David?" I asked.

"That's me."

"It's your cousin Dani here."

He tilted the mirror and looked at me. It had been nearly twenty years since we had last been together at his father's—my uncle Harvey's—funeral. Our fathers were buried next to each other in the Shapiro family plot in Bensonhurst, Brooklyn. The brothers hadn't gotten along, but in death they were together for eternity.

"It's you, all right," David confirmed. His tone was oddly flat. We hadn't known each other particularly well as children. A series of family rifts had kept the cousins apart.

The taxi stopped at a red light.

"Let me come up front," I said, reaching for the door handle.

"No, no—you stay back there."

David was a middle-aged man now. He was also overweight, and looked tired. He had deep purplish circles under his eyes. I searched for traces of the handsome boy I remembered.

"Do you remember the name of our great-great-grandfather?" David asked after a minute. "I've been working on a family tree." He went on to explain that his oldest son was about to be bar mitzvahed.

I tried to remember—but I couldn't go beyond the names carved into the tombstones in the family plot.

"His name might be in that film—you know, that film about Poland, when Grampy—"

I hadn't thought of the film—a documentary called *Image Before My Eyes*—in years. It was a history of Jewish shtetl life in Poland before the Holocaust that included some family footage. In the 1930s our grandfather had made a pilgrimage to his ancestral shtetl, bringing with him one of the early home motion-picture cameras. As a college freshman, I had gone to see the film when it opened in New York. I sat in the darkness of the theater, watching a grainy black-and-white scene of my grandfather and great-grandfather saying the Mourner's Kaddish at the foot of our great-great-grandfather's grave in a Polish village that surely no longer existed.

"I think I have a copy at home," I said. "Give me your address and I'll send it to you."

We lapsed into silence. Small talk seemed out of the question. Our common ground was an empty landscape, littered with misunderstanding and loss that had nothing to do with either of us. As we inched downtown on Fifth Avenue, I thought about that tower high above Central Park. I could hear the sound my shoes made on the marble floors. I could smell the leather desk blotter in my grandfather's study. I thought about my grandfather—buried along with his two sons in the Brooklyn cemetery—and wondered what he would make of his ten grandchildren, who had scattered far and wide, creating their own tribes like the children of Genesis. Some of us had prospered, and some were struggling. Among us were a commercial builder, an acupuncturist, a taxi driver, a computer programmer, an Orthodox rabbi, a businessman, a psychoanalyst, two housewives, and a novelist. My grandfather's patriarchal spell did not extend itself into my generation. There was nothing keeping us together. Had it been inevitable that we lose track of one another? That our children would be strangers?

We pulled up in front of HBO. David carefully wrote his name and address on a scrap of paper and handed it to me. I reached for my wallet. I didn't know what to do. What was the etiquette here?

"Put that away." David waved his hand. I noticed a thick gold wedding ring, and hoped that he was happy. "Please—it's on me."

I climbed out of the taxi and walked around to the driver's

side window. Then he rolled it down. I leaned in to give my cousin a kiss. I wondered if we would ever see each other again.

23.

I have become intimate with a stand of trees in our front meadow. Grouped together near a crumbling stone wall, they are old and stately. On a sturdy branch of a maple extending out toward the driveway, Jacob's rope swing hangs, swaying in the slightest breeze. Halfway through my yoga practice, after the sun salutations and twists and inversions and side angles, I look out my bedroom window as I do a variation of tree pose. *Fix your gaze*, yoga teachers say. *Soften your eyes.* These two instructions seem contradictory. How to fix a gaze softly? How to hold steady and also let go? Standing on one leg, the other foot pressed into my upper thigh, I reach my arms over my head and then—then, I bend. I lean to the side, and allow my head to be dead weight. I forget about the idea of balance. I forget that there is a self who is balancing. I have learned that this is only way that balance is possible. The minute I start thinking about it—*Oh, look at me! Look how far I'm bending today*—I will fall.

All the while, I keep my eyes on the trees. My fixed gaze softens. The stone wall, the sky, the sweep of meadow, go slightly out of focus. This is how I most vividly see the seasons change: in winter, the branches are stark, like charcoal slashes against the gray-white sky; in spring, the reddish cast before the buds appear; in fall, the distracting riot of color; in summer, the lush, verdant thicket. No matter what the season, the trees are bending. They are indifferent to the people who come and go. They were here long before we arrived with our SUVs, our bicycles and rope swings. Their branches are gnarled, knotted, twisted, but still reaching out.

24.

The house in the country was on top of a hill that we would later discover old-timers referred to as Lightning Ridge. A classic New England saltbox painted a weather-beaten gray, it looked out over miles of rolling hills. Stone walls curved along its ten acres of woods and meadow. It was October; the property was aflame. Orange, red, yellow—it seemed that every leaf had turned color but hadn't yet fallen. Halfway down the hill, vines and bramble partially covered what must once have been a tennis court.

It was perhaps the tenth house we'd seen. Michael and I had drawn a geographical circle around New York City. We wanted to be an easy two-hour drive away. What might have seemed an intelligent and informed decision was in fact arrived at by a series of random criteria: I came from New Jersey, and didn't want to go back; Long Island had too much traffic; Westchester was too expensive, and besides, we didn't need to commute, so why live in the suburbs? A good selection of schools was important; were there other young families? Artists? Writers? Democrats? Jews? And what about people's connection to New York? Did they move to the country and slowly but surely abandon city life forever? Did they begin stenciling their walls, making their own quilts? Did they drink too much and have key parties? Everything I knew about the state of Connecticut, I had learned from the novels of Richard Yates and John Cheever, with a bit of Martha Stewart mixed in.

Arthur Miller takes the bus, the real estate agent said, killing four birds—writer, Jew, Democrat, New Yorker—with one stone. The bus being the sole mode of public transportation to New York City. Arthur Miller being a resident of one of the towns in which we were house-hunting. *Arthur Miller takes the bus* became such a frequent refrain that I began to envision a blow-up doll of the great playwright propped up in the back seat of the Bonanza bus from Southbury to the Port Authority.

In truth, Michael and I had no idea what we were doing. We were flying blind—amazed that the proceeds from the sale of our brownstone could buy us these ten acres, this house. It was safety, security, peace of mind, we were after. It had been a rough couple of years. The plain facade of the saltbox, the hand-split wood roof reflecting the autumn light, the gentle slope of the land—it spoke of a simplicity that seemed not only preferable but essential to our family's well-being. But beyond the proximity of Arthur Miller, we knew next to nothing about the place where we were setting down our roots. We were going on instinct. This sense of rightness about the house was a *feeling*—nothing more.

Before we made a final decision to leave the city, we made an appointment for Jacob to see an expert in early childhood development. Jacob's speech was still lagging, and he had been the last of his peer group to learn to walk. The medication he had taken—the stuff that saved his life—had a sedative effect. For a year of his infancy, he had essentially been tranquilized. If he was going to need intervention—speech therapy, occupational therapy, who-knew-what—then maybe we should stay in the city, where I imagined such things were more readily available.

After spending several hours with Jacob doing a comprehensive evaluation, the doctor called us into his office.

"You realize that most children who survive infantile spasms are eventually diagnosed with pervasive developmental disorder," he began. And then—after a brief, sadistic pause: "Jacob is fine. He exhibits no signs of autism."

We moved into the house on a cold, muddy day in early April. I was about to turn forty. Jacob was about to turn three. Michael—heading toward fifty—had switched careers from foreign correspondent to screenwriter. I had spent the previous two years struggling to write a novel. The future was unclear. We had no money to speak of, nothing resembling financial security. Two writers, post–9/11 refugees, strangers in a strange land. We should have been petrified—we should have questioned our own sanity. But we had learned something about what was worth being petrified about, and what wasn't.

25.

The small white leather-bound prayer book is embossed on the inside cover with my parents' names, along with the date and place of their marriage. It has been tucked into the back of a file cabinet drawer for years, along with other mementos of a long-gone life: expired passports, my mother's change purse, my father's old wallet, the velvet pouch that contains his tallit and tefillin. I've rarely opened the file drawer, much less the prayer book itself. I haven't wanted to dwell on my parents as young, hopeful, at the beginning of their lives together.

But I've set myself on a course that doesn't allow me to be a coward. And so recently I pulled the prayer book—along with a few other items—out of the drawer. It sat on my desk for a while before I actually looked inside. There are prayers for everything. Morning Prayer for Boys. Morning Prayer for Girls. Grace after Meals, of course. I could practically hear the well-dressed wedding guests at Young Israel of Fifth Avenue singing the Birkat Hamazon as the last of the strawberry shortcake was cleared from the tables. In the middle of the book, following these more typical prayers, there is a list of "Blessings on Various Occasions":

Before eating bread.

Before drinking wine.

Before partaking of food, other than bread, prepared from any of the five species of grain: wheat, barley, rye, oats, and spelt.

On partaking of meat, fish, eggs, cheese, etc., or drinking any liquor except wine.

On eating fruit that grows on trees.

On eating fruit that grows on the ground, herbage, etc.

On smelling fragrant woods or barks.

On putting on a new garment.

On placing a mezuzah on the doorpost.

On eating any fruit for the first time in season, on entering into possession of a new house or land, on purchasing new dishes.

On witnessing lightning, or on seeing falling stars, lofty mountains, or great deserts.

On hearing thunder or storms.

On seeing the rainbow.

At the first sight of an ocean or sea.

On hearing sad tidings.

On meeting a friend for the first time since his convalescence from sickness.

This last one reads: *Blessed be the Merciful One, who hath given thee back to us, and not given thee unto dust.*

26.

The summer after we first moved to Connecticut, we were invited to a barbecue by the lake. Families from Jacob's school, people we didn't yet know, gathered around grills, coolers filled with ice, tonic, gin, wine, sodas. As the sun set over the lake, little kids splashed in the shallow water along the beach, and bigger kids played freeze-tag as the grown-ups cooked and drank.

I saw a boy—he must have been seven or eight—running around with the others. He looked like Samson, his raggedy mane of blond hair reaching all the way down his skinny back to his waist. This was Connecticut, not Berkeley. The boy stood out.

One of the women saw me notice him, and filled me in. "He was very sick as a baby," she said. "He very nearly died. His parents became born-again. They made a promise to God that if he saved their son, they would never cut his hair, until he was old enough to cut it himself."

I watched the boy whooping it up with his friends. His parents, who had been pointed out to me, were a good-looking couple, blond and rangy. The wife leaned back on a beach chair, balancing a gin and tonic on one tanned knee. It would be years before I exchanged a single word with her, but still—born-again Christian that she was, lapsed Jew that I was—I felt like I knew her. I searched the shoreline for Jacob, my toddler. He was crouched down, examining a rock, his back curved, as if in supplication.

27.

When we were still living in Brooklyn I craved comfort food and cooked it every night. My favorite was a recipe for meat lasagna that included a cup and a half of heavy cream. Also high on the list was spaghetti carbonara: bacon, garlic, eggs, and more heavy cream. I wasn't concerned about calories or fat content. Only with flavor, texture, satisfaction. We opened bottles of good red wine usually reserved for special occasions. Dipped hunks of crusty French bread into leftover sauce. Cleaned our plates. Ate dessert.

During the days, I had begun to work on an assignment for the *New York Times Magazine*. Jacob had spent one night when he was ill under observation in the pediatric step-down intensive care unit at Mount Sinai Hospital—the hospital on the Upper East Side where both he and I had been born. The ward was filled with very sick kids, most of whom lived there. Two girls were awaiting heart transplants; the older one had been in the hospital for nearly a year. A seven-year-old boy lived along with his stuffed animals inside an isolation tent with tubes coming out of his stomach. The halls and doors of the step-down unit were decorated with the children's art projects: watercolors of rainbows, stick-figure drawings of families. Some of the rooms were equipped with video monitors so that the children could communicate with their parents at home.

While Jacob dozed, I had wandered the halls, talking with some of the kids. During the months that followed, I often found myself thinking about them. Eventually—after Jacob was well again—I called an editor at the *Times* and got an assignment to write a story. I started spending all my days at the hospital. I wore a special volunteer identification tag—though everyone on the unit knew I was there as a reporter—and made my way in and out of the children's rooms. I sat in on their tutoring sessions, hovered in their doorways as the doctors made their rounds. The two heart-transplant girls had become close. The eleven-year-old took me aside one day. Her long dark hair streamed in waves down the back of her pink bathrobe. Her eyes were huge and brown.

"It's hard to live here in the hospital, but do you know what? I feel really bad for my friend," she told me. "She's only nine. She hasn't had much of a childhood yet."

There in the step-down unit was the invisible veil that separates the healthy from the sick. It was impossible to be in that hospital ward full of children and push thoughts of Jacob from my mind.

I remembered the way that very same veil had settled over us, like the sheerest netting, just a year and a half earlier. On that long ride home to Brooklyn from the neurologist's office, I had looked out the car window at the Brooklyn Bridge, a sight that had always made my heart lift. Now, my heart was a stone in my chest. The water below was gray, churning. The cars surrounding us were filled with lucky people going about their daily business. They were thinking about what to pick up for dinner, or an annoying thing a colleague said at work. They had no idea how good they had it. And we—we had crossed over to a place where only one thing mattered. *Seven out of a million.* My consciousness, the whole way I saw the world, had been changed in an instant.

I saw Jacob in the face of every child in the step-down unit. I saw Michael and myself in the stooped shoulders of each parent pacing the halls. We had come so close to devastation. We had been dangled by our feet over an abyss—and then brought back. Our veil had lifted—but I knew the truth, which was that the veil hovers, always. It can descend on anyone, at any time. The trick— if it is a trick—is to know this but not let it stop you.

The nurses at Mount Sinai Hospital were the most exhausted nurses I had ever seen. Their patients didn't just come and go, as they would in any other intensive care unit. They came and *stayed,* these children, with their malformed hearts and kidneys and livers. They stayed and—through the daily act of care, the cleaning and disinfecting and flushing of bedpans and stents and intravenous lines—the nurses came to love them. Those nurses knew the odds: at least half of those children wouldn't make it. The clock was always ticking. Donor organs wouldn't arrive in time. A delicate apparatus would falter, then fail. But still—knowing what they knew—they didn't hold back. They opened themselves up to the probability that their hearts would be broken again and again.

One morning, a few weeks into the reporting, I commuted from Brooklyn to the Upper East Side, as I had every other morning. I walked uptown on Fifth Avenue and into the Mount Sinai lobby. The guard knew me by now, and waved me through. But I couldn't get into the elevator, couldn't press the button for the sixth floor. I sat in a plastic chair and waited to feel stronger. I felt like I might come apart—my skin dissolving, with nothing to protect me. I waited in the lobby for a while—that same lobby that I had walked through as a woman in labor, and walked through again with my healthy infant bundled into a car seat. But the feeling didn't pass. I turned around and went home.

I called my editor at the *Times* and told her that I couldn't do the story—I just couldn't do it. These were families who had it so much worse than we ever did, even in our darkest hour. But I had no journalistic distance. Even with my volunteer badge on, striding in from the outside, I wasn't an outsider. I couldn't simply come and go. Each time I left the step-down unit and reentered the land of the lucky, my inner voice screamed: *Why them and not us? Why such terrible maladies? Why should children suffer? Why have we been spared? Why, why, why?*

Months later, I called one of the nurses in the step-down unit to ask about the heart transplant girls. The eleven-year-old had received a heart, and died during surgery. The nine-year-old, alone in the hospital without her friend, was still waiting.

And so I continued to cook. I bought heavy cast-iron cas-
seroles in bright, cheery colors: canary yellow, royal blue. Stews
bubbled on the stovetop. Braised beef, lamb shanks, chicken with
hot spicy sausage. Handmade pasta stuffed with a mixture of
cheese and black trumpet mushrooms. Michael and I gained ten
pounds between us. I clipped recipes, shopped at farmers markets,
tracked down rare ingredients. Small terra-cotta pots of herbs
lined my kitchen windowsill like toy soldiers. Music played. The
back door flung open to the garden below. Jacob toddled around
the kitchen, banging wooden spoons. The wafting scent of siz-
zling garlic, sauteed onions, lured Michael from his third-floor
study. *Daddy! Family hug!* Jacob had learned to say. *Family hug!* his
high sweet voice called out. Day after day, Michael hoisted Jacob
up in his arms, and the three of us held each other in a tight embrace. All the while, far above our Brooklyn brownstone, the veil
floated in the sky.

28.

After returning home from Kripalu, I promised myself that each
day I would practice *metta* meditation for at least fifteen minutes.
Having been on retreat for three days, I didn't think this was a particularly tall order. Surely I had the discipline to sit still for fifteen
minutes. To prepare, I ordered an elaborate meditation cushion,
and a timer that was supposed to chime with the sound of Ti-
betan bells. The meditation cushion with its three-legged plastic
base shaped like a flying saucer proved uncomfortable and strange;

the timer's chimes sounded like the electronic ring of a regular alarm clock. So I gave up on props and tried to just sit, using the comforting *metta* phrases that Sylvia Boorstein had taught.

May I feel protected and safe; may I feel contented and pleased . . . My mind would break through the words almost instantly. *Gotta call the dentist. When's the school picnic?* These first thoughts were all on the level of the utterly mundane. I tried to be a neutral observer—to simply watch the thoughts as if they were clouds in the sky—but it was difficult. I was full of self-judgment. This was what was in my mind? My first layer of consciousness felt like a trash can full of Post-its and to-do lists.

May my physical body support me with strength; may my life unfold smoothly with ease. I couldn't get all the way through these four brief phrases without some bit of detritus from my daily life intruding. *Why hasn't that health insurance reimbursement come in yet?* It seemed impossible to quiet down. Again and again, I was overcome by an intense desire to open my eyes, to move, to check the timer—to stop. The desire felt physical—an uncomfortable surge of energy. As soon as one passed, another would start up again.

On some days I discovered that I was able to tolerate these surges of energy for at least a little while. And when I did, I began to see the endless, circular monologue beneath them. No wonder I didn't want to go there! Worry, fear, doubt, resentment, envy, anxiety, comparison, sadness—apparently these were the themes of the complicated stories churning through my head. Rather than being like a still, clear pool of water—an image often used in visualizations—my mind was a stagnant pond badly in need of dredging. The checklists and tasks were the debris floating on the surface. Either way, it was murky territory, and I didn't want to go there.

But go there I continued to do—because really, what was the alternative? I had gotten a peek at the enemy, and she was me. If worry, fear, doubt, resentment, et al. were part of the fabric of my inner life, didn't I need to know about it? Each day it took longer and longer to prepare myself to meditate; simply plunking myself down on the floor wasn't going to do the trick. I started to worry that this was becoming a full-time job. What was an ambitious, sociable, urban-oriented forty-five-year-old woman doing, spending her mornings sitting in dead silence with her eyes closed in a house in the middle of nowhere?

After Jacob was off to school and Michael had left for his writing studio in town, I unrolled my yoga mat. Most mornings I didn't feel like doing this, but I had learned that it was best to ignore what I *felt* like doing, and instead create a ritual, a habit. I put on the decidedly unorthodox yogic mixed tape that Michael had made me: an eclectic combination of everything from Pink to Leonard Cohen. And then I did my intense hour-long physical practice, which had begun to feel, to me, like the only possible preparation for meditation. It seemed that I needed to physically exhaust myself before my mind could find any quiet.

Once the final strains of k. d. lang singing "Hallelujah" faded away, I was ready—or at least as ready as I could make myself. I folded my legs into half-lotus and began the internal struggle to let go. I repeated Sylvia's phrases. Focused on the out breath. Focused on the in *and* the out breath. Became aware of the birds chirping outside my window, the distant rumble of a truck straining uphill. What *was* this exploration? I was like a scientist experimenting in a laboratory of the self. I watched the thoughts come, tried to label them simply as thinking.

Why did she do that to me? I never—

Thinking.

How are we ever going to be able to afford—

Thinking.

I hope he didn't think that I—

Thinking.

The surges of energy continued. By now, I knew that these surges meant that there was more; beneath these painful, but still mostly mundane, concerns lurked something pure and deep that this simple process of sitting was stirring up. I couldn't touch it yet. All I knew was that sitting helped—and by that, I don't mean that it helped make me feel better. Let me be perfectly clear: meditation was not helping me feel better. It was hard, scary, and sometimes felt silly. What was I doing? I had deadlines to meet. Students to teach. Food shopping to do. But it was helping me to make out the vaguest beginning of an outline. I was starting to see what was there.

29.

My parents had been driving home on a New Jersey highway during an early-evening blizzard when my father passed out behind the wheel. His foot became dead weight and pressed the gas pedal to the floor. His body slumped forward. My mother screamed and lunged over him, trying to steer as the car made two wide circles across the entire width of the highway. It flew over the median, into three lanes of onrushing traffic and back again. By the time the car crashed into a concrete embankment and came to a stop, my mother had sustained eighty fractures. Her right leg was shattered, she had multiple broken ribs, a broken nose, a lacerated cheekbone. She was bleeding internally. My father was unconscious. It took two and a half weeks for him to die.

I have often wondered what I was doing at the exact moment of my parents' accident. I might have been sleeping, or lying in bed reading a magazine. I might have been sipping a cup of tea. How could I not have felt it happening? I was on the other side of the country, in southern California, but still—how does the fabric that connects us rip into shreds without our knowing it? The day of my parents' accident, I had the only allergic reaction I've ever had to anything before or since. Hives covered my face and upper body. I became hot, itchy, swollen—as if some foreign creature had become trapped inside me and was desperately trying to claw its way out. Coincidence? Probably. But it's hard not to feel that my body knew something that the rest of me didn't.

30.

I stood on the front stoop of my aunt Shirley's gray-and-white Tudor house in Brookline, Massachusetts, and tried to pull myself together before knocking. Shirley—my father's younger sister—was now in her mid-eighties, and had lived here for over sixty years, since she was a bride. As a child, I barely ever visited; my mother couldn't stand Shirley, and had kept me away. I could practically hear my mother's voice: *Oh, please. That woman only pretends to be pious,* she would say. *She's always so holier-than-thou.*

But now, Shirley was the single existing bridge between my present and my past. Whenever I spoke with her, I was filled with questions. Had my father really been a believer? Or had his observance come from a combination of habit and fear? Why had my mother been so threatened by his family and their religious practices? She used to scornfully refer to them as *a tribe.* Was there something so very wrong with being a tribe?

In the past, though I often thought of spending a weekend in Brookline, I never had. I was too afraid. Afraid of feeling like an outsider in my own family. Afraid of being too different, too modern, too assimilated. Too much my mother's daughter. My first thought on Shabbos morning would be how to sneak out to Starbucks for a venti cappuccino.

I rang the bell. *Shit.* It was Shabbos. I had forgotten, for a second. I shouldn't have pressed a button, shouldn't have set off the chimes inside her darkened house. There was a brass knocker right there in front of my face. Ringing a bell—the transmittal of electricity—was forbidden. How could I have done such a stupid thing? I hadn't even walked inside yet, and already I had done something wrong. More than that—I had underscored the differences between us.

Shirley opened the heavy front door. She looked essentially the same as she always had. Her heart-shaped face was still unlined, and she wore a well-cut, modest skirt and a simple white blouse. Her dark hair was pulled tightly back from her widow's peak and tucked into a bunlike hairpiece.

"Darling"—she didn't blink at the breach of Shabbos—"I'm so happy to see you. Come in, come in."

Earlier that week, Michael and Jacob had scored tickets to a Saturday-afternoon Red Sox game at Fenway Park—just a short trip down Beacon Street from Brookline. My first thought was to go along for the ride, then spend the afternoon visiting my aunt while they went to the game. But when it came to calling Shirley, I had been torn. Would she be uncomfortable about my driving to see her on Shabbos? Would she feel like she had to turn me down—or worse, would she feel obliged to see me out of some Talmudic logic? After all, the Talmud allowed for all sorts of exceptions to the rules. You could drive on Shabbos in a medical emergency. Was there a provision for the nonobservant niece who drives on Shabbos anyway?

Shirley looked up at me, squinting in the sunlight.

"I think you've gotten taller," she said. "Or maybe I've shrunk."

I pulled up the hem of my jeans. "It's the heels."

We walked into her foyer, past the wide, curved staircase. Beneath the banister, on a metal track, my uncle Moe's electrical chairlift sat empty. It had been installed a decade earlier, when Moe first began to deteriorate from Parkinson's disease. Now, at ninety-three, he was upstairs in his bed, intubated and on oxygen. Moe and Shirley lived alone in this house, their children long gone. A solitary beam of sunlight shone through a high window, like an old movie projector in the cool darkness.

Shirley and I sat across from each other on two faded upholstered chairs. On the coffee table, a small pile of books written by family members had a place of honor: *Flames of Faith: An Introduction to Chasidic Thought*, by Rabbi Zev Reichman; *The Right and the Good: Halakhah and Human Relations*, by Daniel Feldman; and a hardcover edition of *Black & White*, my most recent novel, which it would be safe to say was the only contemporary fiction in the house. I mentally skimmed its pages, thinking about disturbing passages, nudity, profanity. I knew Shirley had read it—she had called to compliment me on it when it was published earlier that year—and hoped she hadn't found it too upsetting.

Above the fireplace hung the portrait of my grandfather—it had been transported from Central Park West to Brookline many years before. He peered through his pince-nez, leather-bound book in hand. I imagined, for a moment, that he could see the array of photographs crowded on top of the grand piano. Shirley is the mother of four, grandmother of twenty, and great-grandmother of thirty-two and counting: dozens of boys in yarmulkes, their faces framed by the wispy tendrils of *pais*; girls in formal dresses, lacy white anklets, black patent leather Mary Janes. What would my grandfather think if he saw me, in that room?

"This is the newest addition to the family." Shirley handed me a photo of a young couple—a pale man in a black, wide-brimmed hat and a woman in a shoulder-length wig—holding a new baby. "Ezra's first. A boy."

"And Ezra is—?" I asked. It was hard to keep track.

"Henry's youngest. They're living in Jerusalem," she said. "Both he and his brother Joshua have become Haredim."

I searched Shirley's face for clues as to how she felt about this. The Haredim are the most Orthodox of the Orthodox. This meant that Shirley's grandkids had swung all the way to the outer edges of the religious right. They lived in insular communities, cut off from the outside world, with no television, no radio or secular newspaper. They spent their lives—literally every waking minute of their lives—studying Torah. Her great-grandkids might not even learn to speak English.

"Is that . . . okay?" I asked. "Or is it . . ." I trailed off. Not sure of this territory. Not sure what to say.

"The way I see it, when you get to be my age, you move over into the slow lane," Shirley said. "And you let the next generations whiz by."

How becoming Haredim constituted whizzing by, I wasn't certain. It seemed more like time travel—away from the real world and into a galaxy all its own. The word itself—*haredi*—derives from the Hebrew word for fear. "One who trembles in awe of God." In their eyes, I doubt I would even qualify as Jewish. I fought the intrusion of my mother's voice once again. As was so often the case, I knew exactly what she would think.

"So tell me—" Shirley changed the subject. She leaned forward, her hands clasped. "How is Michael? How is Jacob?"

My family—my husband and son—seemed so small in comparison to the gallery of photographs. So small and so very American.

"They're great," I answered, trying to regain my equilibrium. "Michael's working on a few different screenwriting projects. Jacob's enjoying school."

"And the Red Sox," Shirley said. "Who is his favorite player? I like Manny Ramirez myself."

I wondered how my aunt had managed it. How had she raised

her enormous devout family while still maintaining an active connection to politics, world history, literature, even sports? Not a single one of her children or grandchildren had strayed from religious Orthodoxy. As evidenced by the photographs on her piano, quite a few had gone deeper into it. I looked over at the bookcases on either side of my grandfather's portrait. To his right, Dickens, Melville, Cather. To his left, Maimonides, Theodor Herzl, Schneerson. The secular and the religious, coexisting in a home where Manny Ramirez and Haredim could come up in the same conversation.

Past the abandoned chairlift and up the staircase, the family's patriarch lay on his side in his hospital bed. On the wall outside his room hung photographs of Moe as a vigorous, middle-aged man shaking hands with John Kennedy, Lyndon Johnson. Now, his eyes were half open. His attendant, Bruno, sat in a chair nearby, reading an old copy of *Reader's Digest*.

"Look who's here, Moe—it's Dani!" Shirley said.

I bent down so that Moe and I were face-to-face. Was he conscious? Or not? It was impossible to know. And if he was, would he want to see me? I was the black sheep. Or rather, the blond sheep. The one who drove on Shabbos and worse—much worse.

"Hi, Uncle Moe," I said softly. "It's so good to see you."

I thought I saw a flicker of recognition in those eyes. I wasn't sure if I should touch him. Degrees of Orthodoxy dictate whether men and women—even relatives—are allowed to touch. How is it that I didn't know, after all these years, where he fell on the spectrum?

Shirley moved about the room, checking Moe's oxygen, his medication schedule. I was reminded of all the years I had visited my grandmother after her stroke. Shirley had spent the middle of her life traveling from Boston to New York each week to care for her bedridden mother. Now she was spending her later years nursing her husband in precisely the same way: at home, every need taken care of, loved until the end.

The only sound in the house was the hum of the medical equipment surrounding Moe's bed. *Whoosh*, silence. *Whoosh*, silence. His eyes fluttered closed. The room was in shadows.

"Dani, come see my lady," Shirley called. She stood at the one bright spot, at the window overlooking the small park on the other side of Beech Road.

I joined her at the window, and saw instantly what she meant. The park was full of different kinds of beech trees. In the center of the park, directly across from Shirley's house, was a majestic weeping beech. She—the tree could only be a she—must have towered fifty or sixty feet high. Narrower at the top, her lower branches cascading in waves that appeared to be layers of a skirt, she looked as if she had been there forever.

"How big was that tree when you first moved here?" I asked Shirley.

She shook her head. "Oh, she hadn't even been planted yet."

My aunt put her arm around my shoulders. I had been only half born into this world of ritual and observance, of flames and spices, Hebrew volumes lining bookshelves, blessings for every moment in the day—and, like the stronger of twin animals, the other half had fought and won. Still, my history tugged at me. I tried to imagine what it would be like to spend an entire lifetime in one place. To put down roots—to live in one single spot long enough to see the world sprout up around you. To watch the empty space outside your window become a sapling—and that sapling become an old, stately specimen. To give birth to a village. To be surrounded by the world you've created. To be governed by a belief so strong that nothing—not sadness, nor anger, nor grief—can shake it. To believe in God.

31.

One early spring afternoon, I met Steve Cope for lunch at Cafe Helsinki in Great Barrington, Massachusetts. The cafe, a cozy spot furnished with scarred wooden tables and old sofas piled with comfortable cushions, had become our meeting place between my home in Connecticut and Kripalu. Over tabouli salad and falafel, I tried to express the confusion I had been feeling lately. I told Steve that I felt like I was stumbling along in the darkness. I was reading, thinking, exploring, meditating, practicing yoga. I had discovered gems of wisdom buried here and there. But there didn't seem to be one, well-lit path opening itself up to me, the way I had hoped it might.

I wondered out loud whether this desire of mine for a little bit of this, a little bit of that, was spiritual and intellectual laziness. The smorgasbord approach to deeper meaning. I was reminded of a mom at Jacob's school who posted flyers around town advertising herself as a shamanic healer, dream therapy guide, social worker, and facilitator of interspecies communication honoring

Native American, Buddhist, Kundalini, and Kabbalah influences. Oy vey. How could I give Jacob a spiritual foundation when I was all over the map? Did I have to choose one way? Was that the true discipline?

Steve shrugged, then smiled. His bright blue eyes were sharp, unclouded. He took a sip of his cardamom tea.

"Do you know anything about ayurvedic impressions?" he asked.

I didn't.

"According to ayurveda, we become what we surround ourselves with."

I nodded. That made sense.

"And so it stands to reason that we have to be discerning about what we surround ourselves with."

Discernment. Such a beautiful word. As usual, Steve had cut straight to the heart of the matter. I thought about what it meant to choose wisely—not just once or twice, but in every waking moment.

"Recently I've started going to church," Steve said. This, coming from my friend the yogi, the Buddhist scholar. "After my mother died, I found it brought me comfort. Even though I only believe maybe thirty percent of what I hear in there—I don't believe that Jesus Christ is the one true son of God, which is kind of central—I walk out feeling lighter."

Steve didn't sound remotely confused or apologetic. He could pick and choose what felt relevant to him, and leave the rest. Why couldn't I do the same? When I was in an Orthodox shul, I felt like an imposter: a bacon-and-shrimp-eating fake who could still chant the liturgy like an old tune. When I was in more liberal shuls, I wasn't comfortable either. *Men and women davening together?* *Women wearing prayer shawls?* I saw it all through my father's eyes: women in tallits and yarmulkes looked silly to me, like little girls playing dress-up. And in yoga studios, chanting made me nervous. The Sanskrit words sounded disconcertingly like Hebrew. I had been told that it didn't matter, that the vibrations of the syllables worked their own magic, but still, I felt like I was doing something wrong.

As I sat with my new friend, I realized that perhaps he was doing the hardest thing of all: living inside the contradictions. Buddhism, yoga philosophy, the high Episcopalian tradition in which he had been steeped as a child, were all able to coexist for him and create a greater, richer equilibrium. This wasn't spiritual laziness. To the contrary, it required even greater effort and clarity.

"You know, Dani, you don't have to throw the baby out with the bathwater." Steve leaned across the table. "There's still a baby in there."

32.

I started thinking about the Sabbath. I had been reading Abraham Joshua Heschel's book by that same name, in which he makes a distinction between the world of things and the world of time. *Things, when magnified, are forgeries of happiness,* Heschel wrote. Forgeries of happiness. Had truer words ever been written? I thought of the stuff piled in our closets, spilling out of chests of drawers. Or the way sometimes (okay, often) I coveted some pretty thing I had seen in a shop window—a cashmere sweater, a pashmina wrap.

I was surrounded by the accoutrements of my modern life. From the kitchen table where I sat writing on my laptop each morning, just within my line of vision there was an espresso machine, a separate device to steam milk, bottles of gourmet vinegar, bee pollen, truffle oil. Piles of *New Yorker*s and *Vanity Fair*s, glossy catalogs, party invitations, and save-the-date cards for events scheduled months ahead. A scented candle burned near the stove. I lived in the world of things, and honestly, I didn't want it any other way. I mean, what was I going to do? Check into Kripalu for the duration? Become one of the Haredim, like my cousins? No—I wanted to find a way to live in balance. *Things, when magnified*, Heschel wrote. The problem wasn't the stuff of fast-paced life itself. The problem, he seemed to be saying, was one of emphasis. And the remedy came in the form of the seventh day—the Sabbath.

Heschel described the Sabbath—with its call to slow down, to devote a full day to quiet contemplation—as a cathedral of time. I had never experienced this. The Sabbaths of my childhood had not been cathedrals. They had been exercises in boredom—and also, in coming up with new and ingenious ways to bend the rules. We weren't supposed to turn on lights, but there was a timer that did it for us. It wasn't permitted to switch on the stereo, but my mother had the system rigged so that at two in the afternoon, the opening notes of her weekly opera program would miraculously begin to sound throughout the house. And then, if we happened to be visiting family in the city, there was the Sabbath elevator: in certain buildings, elevators were programmed to stop on every floor on Friday nights and Saturdays so that observant

Jews wouldn't have to push the buttons. How could this possibly be the point?

The higher goal of spiritual living is not to amass a wealth of information, but to face sacred moments, Heschel wrote. I wanted to face sacred moments. I knew that some kind of ritual was, if not essential, certainly useful. And so I began to consider lighting Friday-night candles. It was just one gesture, I told myself. I would gather my family together to do this one simple thing. It didn't have to be the beginning of some slippery slope that would end in cold brisket lunches and desperate, quiet boredom. It was a beautiful tradition: the reciting of the blessing, the circling of cupped hands over the flames, ushering in the Sabbath.

I had the candlesticks from my childhood: tall silver ones from Tiffany that had been a wedding gift to my parents from Shirley and Moe. I moved them from the living room, where they had been a decorative touch, into the dining room. I placed them at the head of the table. I bought a dozen simple white candles. A book of matches was laid out and ready. Friday evening came and went. Then another. And another. The candles remained unlit. Homework got in the way. We had a dinner reservation. The Red Sox game was on TV. Each week, in the battle between things and time, things kept winning.

33.

In my twenties, I spent several hours a week in church basements. I sat on metal folding chairs in smoke-filled rooms and attended hundreds of meetings of Alcoholics Anonymous. Oh, how I loved Alcoholics Anonymous! I was a lost, sad, lonely girl who drank to excess—who did *everything* to excess—and in those church basements I felt safe and cozy, like a wayfarer coming in out of the cold.

My father had recently died. My mother was in a rehabilitation center, where she was slowly learning to walk again. Before my parents' accident—and much to their dismay—I had dropped out of college to pursue a career in acting. It wasn't going well. Each day I put on my makeup, fluffed up my hair, and dragged myself to auditions for bit parts on soap operas. I didn't know which was worse: getting the jobs, or not getting them. If I got a part, it meant I actually had to act. I was a terrible, self-conscious actress. Still, people sometimes hired me. On my agent's suggestion, I adopted a stage name: Dani York. Instantly I became a generic blonde of indeterminate origins. Casting directors often asked me if I was the British actress Susanna York's daughter.

In Alcoholics Anonymous, during those years, I found my sanctuary. People came from every walk of life. They were rich, poor, young, middle-aged, elderly. They were Christian, Jewish, Catholic. (You didn't tend to see many Muslims.) The only requirement for membership was a desire to stop drinking—and I did have a desire to stop drinking. I had a desire to stop a lot of things. I had spent so much of my life adhering to a strict set of rules, and then rebelling against them. I had no idea who I really was—but I wanted to find out. And in order to do that, I needed a clear head.

I had a little problem, though. I wasn't sure I could deal with the God stuff. That word—God—was everywhere in the program literature. It was invoked four times in the twelve steps alone. The third step read: "Made a decision to turn our will and our lives over to the care of God as we understood him." I had turned my will and my life over to God practically since the day I was born, and I wasn't so keen on doing it now. And while I appreciated the "as we understood him" part, the truth was that I didn't understand him. The God of my childhood was a man with a white beard in the sky who judged and found us wanting, who meted out punishment and responded only to heavy-duty petitioning and praise. And look what had happened to my father! He had played by the rules, and had been struck down in the middle of his life. How was that fair or just? What could God possibly have meant by doing that?

There was also the small matter of the Lord's Prayer. Most AA meetings began or ended with everyone shuffling to their feet, clasping hands, closing eyes, and reciting the most popular of all Christian prayers: *Our father who art in Heaven, hallowed be thy name* . . . Even though I had walked (okay, run) away from the God of my childhood—even though I didn't believe in him—he still scared the shit out of me. What would he do to a Jewish girl who had changed her name to York and recited the Lord's Prayer?

Despite these incongruities, I stayed sitting on my metal folding chair, day after day, week after week. I went to meetings in high-ceilinged rooms in Episcopal churches, musty basements of rectories downtown. I attended meetings in other cities: Los Angeles, Paris, London. I felt the way people with strong religious affiliations must: at home anywhere in the world. Equipped with a list of meetings, I could find a place any hour of the day where I would be welcomed with open arms.

If pressed, I would have said that I didn't think I was an alcoholic. I had been drinking too much, to be sure. But drinking wasn't actually the problem. Occasionally I shared this sneaking suspicion with a fellow member, who would smile at me kindly and suggest that I keep coming back. The implication was that if I was at an AA meeting, I de facto belonged there. And it was true—despite all my self-doubts and guilt about the God stuff—I was comforted by a sense of belonging that I had never experienced before.

I didn't mind calling myself an alcoholic. It was the price of admission. I would have called myself a two-headed turtle if it meant I could keep showing up at meetings. I felt allied with these people who were all trying to get better. I was trying to get better too. I was looking for a structure, a system, a way to live my life. Putting down booze was the least of it. And besides, no one's life has ever gotten worse by *not* drinking.

Many of the twelve steps made sense to me. *Made a searching and fearless moral inventory of ourselves.* You couldn't go wrong with that, really. *Made a list of all persons we had harmed, and became willing to make amends to them all.* Seemed like a pretty good idea. Living life based on a series of instructions developed by two recovering alcoholics—Bill Wilson and Doctor Bob—felt more relevant, more applicable to my daily life, than the accumulated knowledge from all my years in the yeshiva.

Each day I tuned in, mesmerized by the stories people told. Those meetings taught me, for the first time in my life, that people's outsides didn't always match their insides. A beautifully turned-out, poised woman broke down weeping over how her drinking had ruined her relationship with her now-grown children. A hip-looking man with a scruffy beard talked about ending up in a state mental institution, destitute and friendless. The stories were often harsh and painful, but there was redemption in the very fact that the teller had lived to tell the tale. It was never too late to begin again. The human heart was elastic. It could withstand untold grief and still keep beating.

I didn't belong there—I didn't have any right to be there, really—but still I stayed. I stayed for years. Sometimes AA felt like a fellowship. Other times, like a cult—with its own language, its own set of rules. But either way, something was happening in those meetings—something I had longed for but couldn't have named. I now know it was a kind of grace. As much as I had tried to leave God out of it, once in a while, as I looked around any given dingy church basement, it would occur to me that perhaps this *was* God. Not the terrifying gray-bearded figure of my youth. Not the heavenly father from the Lord's Prayer. But right here, in the eloquence rising out of despair, the laughter out of darkness. The nodding heads, the clasping hands. The kindness extended to strangers. The sense—each and every time—of *Me too, I've been there too.* Never before had I listened so carefully or learned so much.

34.

We took a drive—the three of us—up north, into the Berkshire Hills on a random Sunday. We like to do this sometimes: drive an hour or two, making stops in Great Barrington at the cheese store, the Japanese restaurant, the candy store. Sometimes we play mini golf. Other times—much to Jacob's dismay—we pull into an antiques shop to poke around. On this particular Sunday, the leaves had begun to turn.

Autumn has always been my favorite season, and even more so since we've moved to a part of the country known for its foliage. As we drove past lakes framed with the fiery mix of color, I had a familiar desire to freeze the moment—to stop time. *Stay this way*, I silently asked. I wasn't just asking the leaves to hold on to the trees. I was asking Jacob to stay a little boy, for Michael to remain vital and healthy, for myself to stay a while longer in this chapter of my life.

"Mommy?" Jacob piped up from the back seat. "I'm hungry. Is there anything to eat or drink?"

Even this—even my son calling me Mommy—felt bittersweet. When would I be demoted to just plain Mom?

I reached into the back seat and handed Jacob a bag of chips and a milk box. I was longing for the moment I was in, even as I was in it. I was mourning it, as if we were already a yellowed photograph in an album: my family together on a country drive, young, healthy, happy, whole.

I knew better, of course. I knew that trying to capture time—to hold on to anything at all—was not only useless, but a terrible waste. Time was all we had. I had carried with me Heschel's idea of time as a cathedral. It didn't have to be Sabbath for this moment to be holy. It was holy precisely because there was no other.

We stopped at MASS MoCA, a museum in North Adams, Massachusetts, where we met a couple of friends and sat outside on that glorious fall day. We had brought our new puppy along with us for the ride. Jacob and the pup tromped through the dried leaves together. It was almost too much for me—the crispness of the air, the cloudless sky, our friends, my husband's hand in mine, the boy and his pup. The impossible bounty, the moment overflowing.

Let me feel this, I found myself thinking—asking, wishing. Or maybe even praying, if this was praying. *Let me live inside this cathedral of time.* I didn't want to think about the latest newspaper headlines, or what had happened yesterday, or might happen tomorrow. I just wanted to feel the warmth of Michael's hand, listen to Jacob shriek with delight.

It was then that I looked above me, and realized that we were sitting in the midst of an art installation. Suspended high over-head were six cylindrical aluminum planters hanging upside down by wires. They hung from an armature made of steel telephone poles. Out of each planter, a tree grew downward. These trees were not small. Their trunks must have been eighteen inches around. They had clearly been growing this way for quite some time—perhaps years. Their leaves were a rich, autumnal red. They hung in what seemed a precarious way. It looked, in equal parts, beautiful and wrong. How could the trees continue to thrive? But wait—there was something more. As I adjusted to the sight of the dangling trees, I saw that they had begun to shift shape, their branches bending and twisting, so that they could grow away from the earth and back up toward the sky.

Jacob ran over to us, breathless from his romp with the pup. His sturdy little body leaned into Michael and me. The sight of those strange, displaced trees contorting themselves had forced me fully into the present. I felt it all, all at once—the way that time can slow to a near standstill simply by existing inside it. By not pushing through it, or past it—by not wishing it away, nor trying to capture it. It was a lesson I needed to learn over and over again: to stop and simply be. To recognize these moments and enter them—with reverence and an unprotected heart—as if walking into a cathedral.

35.

I didn't write during the year that Jacob was sick. Writing was my job, but I had no office, no time clock, no schedule, no boss breathing down my neck. Writing was how Michael and I both made a living—but now, neither of us could concentrate on anything other than making our baby well again. As if it was up to us. As if we might, if only we were smart enough, resourceful enough, brave enough, good enough, be able to reach into the future and fix things with our own bare hands.

Our days were defined by the five doses of powdery, white experimental medication. We tore open packets of the stuff, cut it into even lines, then sprinkled it onto baby food, or mixed it into formula. If Jacob spit up even a little bit, it was potentially catastrophic. Had the medicine been digested? Should we re-dose him? With the help of the pediatric neurologist, we were making it up as we went along. This wasn't an exact science—but there was also no room for error.

The rest of the time, I sat in front of my computer, not writing. Instead, I spent hours on the Internet looking for references to infantile spasms. There were Web rings, parental support groups, photographs of blind, deaf, physically and mentally impaired children. Parents told their stories: a three-year-old who had finally taken a single step; a five-year-old who had managed to wave. With each click of my mouse, I entered into a whole new world of pain.

I could tell, during that time, who among our friends and family had done the same research. I could tell by the looks on their faces when they saw us. It was something beyond concern. It was pity. They had seen those same photographs. They had called doctor friends. They had heard the unrelentingly bad news, the cold, hard statistics. And they believed that Jacob was lost to us. I couldn't even look these well-meaning friends in the eye.

Not us, not us, not us. It was the drumbeat by which I lived my life. I couldn't stop reading, even though it made me feel worse. I needed to know everything, to stare directly into the monstrous face of this disease that was threatening to steal our son away from us. We were going to lick this thing—we had to. I had never been much of a fighter; it simply wasn't my temperament. But now, my vision narrowed. My claws sharpened. I was a warrior, fighting for every bit of knowledge that could possibly help.

Fifteen percent of babies diagnosed with infantile spasms had positive outcomes. We were looking to be part of that tiny minority within the even tinier minority of babies stricken. *Fifteen percent of seven out of a million.* Statistically speaking, it was a bit like buying a lottery ticket expecting to win.

Every day, I took Jacob to a play group, or the park, or a Mommy & Me class. I figured if I kept things seeming normal, maybe they would eventually become normal. I sat in circles with other mothers, bouncing him on my lap while singing, "If you're happy and you know it clap your hands." I put him on wooden play sets and in sandboxes with other babies, and hovered in a maternal cluster nearby. Most of us carried state-of-the-art diaper bags outfitted with compartments for bottles and blankets and changing pads. The conversation was a hallucinatory swirl of pre-school waiting lists, the benefits of breast-feeding, the medicaliza-tion of childbirth, family bed versus Ferberizing. I dug my hand into my jeans pocket to be sure that I had a packet of medication with me in case we got stuck somewhere. I lived in fear of missing a dose by even fifteen minutes.

I couldn't stop comparing. As the months went by, one by one, like birds flying out of a nest, the babies in his play group began to pull themselves up, to toddle a few steps—everything the authors of *What to Expect* said they were supposed to be able to do. They pointed, clapped, strung together words. *Should be able to, may be able to, might even be able to*—the owner's manual to my child continually scrolled like a newsfeed through my head. One day, a perky Mommy & Me instructor told me that Jacob lacked upper body strength, and I should try to get him to do push-ups. I wept as I pushed his stroller home.

For the first time, I understood why the Adlers had closed their doors to me, all those years before. They couldn't stand seeing me before them, healthy and fully alive—the very embodiment of everything their daughter would never be again. It wasn't a failure of character. It was a complete and utter defeat of hope.

But I refused to lose hope. Every day, when not entertaining fantasies about applying to medical school (if there was a more useless occupation than novelist, I was hard-pressed to come up with it), I searched for stories with happy endings. On the Internet, there were none. I had heard one story, though: a friend offered to put me in touch with a woman he knew whose son had been diagnosed with infantile spasms many years before. That son had recently graduated from Dartmouth. Dartmouth! I couldn't wait to talk to this woman. I longed for a story about a boy with infantile spasms who ended up at a great school. A few days later, my friend called me back. His voice was grim.

"I'm sorry. I don't understand it, but she doesn't want to talk to you. That time in her life was too painful. She can't bear reliving it."

"Not even to—"

"I'm sorry. No."

I will never be her, I silently vowed. One more item on the list. *If Jacob is part of that fifteen percent, I will never, ever be her.*

36.

These days, my conversations with people invariably turn to God. I have friends who call themselves atheists or agnostics. Friends who are believers. But the majority of people I know fall into a gray area, a category I would call the disenchanted. *I can't believe in a God who would*—fill in the blank. Allow the genocides in Rwanda, Srebrenica, Darfur, to happen. Allow the Asian tsunami. Allow loved ones to die suddenly, tragically. The bottom line: How could God condone—or possibly create—so much suffering in the world? If God exists, he's either indifferent to our pain, or sadistically inflicting it. *I refuse to believe in a God like that,* they say.

Did God save Jacob's life? If God saved Jacob's life, then it stands to reason that it was God who gave Jacob the seizure disorder to begin with. After all, we can't pick and choose, can we? Something bad happens, there is no God. Something good happens, we thank him. If I were to believe that God was personally responsible for Jacob's recovery, I'd also have to believe that he caused it. *Seven out of a million.* Why would he do that—to us, to anybody? When Jacob was sick, a well-meaning but dim-witted stranger offered my least favorite platitude: *God doesn't give us more than we can handle.* Our child recovered. So did that mean that God didn't think we could handle the dire consequences of Jacob's illness? Thank you, God. But wait. Wait a minute. What about all those other babies? Had God felt that their parents were more equipped to deal with a lifetime of unending grief?

As I was sitting at my kitchen table trying to untangle the Gordian knot of all this, a friend called to tell me a story. Earlier that day, she had trailered her horse up to a nature preserve along with her teenage daughter and the daughter's friend. They drove her huge rig along the steep, narrow roads of our town, around winding curves, straining up inclines until they arrived at the flat field where the horse trailers park. At that moment, when she tried to stop, the rig's brakes failed. If it had happened on the way to their destination, surely they all—my friend, her daughter, her daughter's friend, the horse—would have been killed. My friend went on to tell me that she had spent the rest of the day feeling very grateful to God. She felt that he had offered her protection. She gave other examples of times in her life during which God had supplied similar protection. Clearly, she felt that God was watching out specifically for her.

I was relieved that my friend was home safe—but something about her story was rubbing me the wrong way. *Oh, so God singled you out for good fortune? For being on the right side of near misses? For specialness?* To distract myself, I clicked on the *New York Times* Web site. Six Iraqis were killed by a roadside bomb hours earlier. A fire had blazed through a Brooklyn building, killing an entire family. A child had been abducted in the Midwest. I didn't believe that God had a hand in that day's tragic events—any more than I believed that he had steered my friend's rig to safety. I didn't believe that God had stopped Jacob's seizures, or that God had caused my father to pass out behind the wheel of his car. I didn't believe that God considered what people could or could not handle. Still, I said *thank you* and *please* into the thin air. I prayed for the willingness to pray—not to an indifferent God, certainly not to a punishing and vengeful God, not to a God who was watching out for me—but to the God I felt all around me, the more I looked.

37.

Sometimes it feels as if I'm building a bridge. This act of bridge-building requires stamina, balance, and more strength than I think I possess. What's more, I have to walk fairly far out onto the bridge as I'm building it. At this point, I'm way out there—too far to make it back to land if the bridge starts to splinter. Sometimes it sways. Once in a while, I hear it creaking. Below me, a precipitous drop: a rock-filled ravine. Best not to look down. Best to put one foot in front of the other. *Krama akrama*, the Sanskrit teaching goes: *Step by step and all at once.* I guess there's only one way to get to the other side: best to have faith.

38.

My cousin Mordechai—Shirley's oldest son—has seven children. One or another of them always seems to getting married. Large cream-colored envelopes arrive with some regularity in the morning mail, addressed in ornate, swirling calligraphy: *Mr. & Mrs. Michael Marrens. Mr. & Mrs. Michael Marin. Mr. & Mrs. Michael Marron.* It's become a joke between Michael and me. Even though my family has no trouble with names like Avshalom or Nechemya, they still can't get my husband's surname, which is Maren, right. Inside, the invitations are engraved in both English and Hebrew. The ceremonies are held at facilities in Orthodox enclaves like Monsey, New York, or sometimes Jerusalem. The wedding date is generally only a couple of weeks away; no long engagements for young couples who have never once been alone together, never so much as touched hands.

A recent invitation threw me into a mini-crisis. Mordechai's third daughter was getting married. This wedding was being held only a couple of hours' drive from us, on a night we happened to be free. We had no legitimate excuse not to go, really. But still, when it came to sending in the reply card, I was paralyzed. Declining made me feel sad and alone. Accepting meant entering the universe of my family and their customs, which sometimes had the power to make me feel even more deeply sad and alone. How could I be related to this group of people, when our lives were so radically different?

But I was trying to understand where—if anywhere—all this fit into my own Jewishness, wasn't I? How could I even pretend to be exploring these matters if I wasn't willing to be made a little uncomfortable? Sylvia Boorstein's words echoed through my mind, where she seemed to have taken up permanent residence: *It's not a question, for me, of deciding to complicate myself with Judaism. I am complicated with Judaism. I have too much background in it not to be.*

Complicated with it, indeed. A few weeks later, Michael and I made the trip to Monsey, and parked outside a shiny pink building. We sat in the car for a few minutes, watching bearded men in black coats pass by. The bride was having her photograph taken. She looked beautiful, impossibly young. Was she eighteen? Nineteen? She was surrounded by girls wearing modest dresses, women in perfect wigs. They looked so familiar to me. Some of them were probably relatives. The family had expanded so rapidly I could no longer keep track. Babies were born and had grown up while I was busy doing other things. The couple who had gotten married at the last family wedding we'd attended now had five kids of their own.

"I'm not going to dance." Michael stared straight ahead as we continued to sit in the car. Neither of us were ready to make a move.

"Don't worry, honey. You won't have to dance."

"You said that last time."

"Last time was twelve years ago!"

"Yeah, but still. It was traumatic."

It was true. Michael—at the time he was my boyfriend—had

made me promise that he wouldn't have to dance. Under *normal* circumstances, dancing wasn't his favorite activity; even dancing with me usually involved a couple of whiskeys. But what was I supposed to do when my cousins Henry, Mordechai, and Jonathan had converged on Michael and picked him up out of his seat by the back of his jacket? The next thing I knew, he was surrounded by a vortex of sweaty men lifting each other up on chairs high above their heads.

The parking lot was filling up. We left the cocoon of our car and slowly walked toward the shiny, pink marble building. The black-hat crowd milled outside the two arched entrances framed by gold Hebrew lettering: apparently men and women weren't even allowed to walk inside together. But then I saw, beyond the doors, that there was pre-ceremony mingling going on in the lobby.

"I don't have a yarmulke," Michael whispered, once we were both inside. I looked around for a basket. Usually there was a basket of yarmulkes. But then I realized that none of these men would ever find themselves without one.

With Michael's bare head, my obvious lack of wig, and perhaps most of all my bare legs beneath my knee-length dress, I knew we looked as if we had made a wrong turn somewhere around the George Washington Bridge. We had stumbled into the wrong party. Where were we going to find him a yarmulke?

"Excuse me." A couple walked up to us. I had noticed them in the parking lot. They had driven a Volvo with Vermont license plates and looked like New England academics, as out of place in this crowd as we were.

"Do you know if men and women are seated separately?" the woman asked.

I told her I was quite sure we would be seated separately. After all, we hadn't even entered the building through the same door.

"What about for the ceremony?" she went on.

Same deal. Men on one side, women on the other. I felt good about myself, filling this poor woman in on the rites and rituals with which I was familiar. See? I did belong here. I could be part of it—I could claim it as a piece of myself, no matter how small.

"You know"—she inclined her head toward me conspiratorially—"we're so relieved that there are other non-Jewish people at this wedding."

39.

Closure (business): the process by which an organization ceases operations

Closure (computer science): an abstraction binding a function to its scope

Closure (psychology): a state of experiencing an emotional conclusion to a difficult life event, or, a point in the development of an artifact where social understanding and interpretation reaches consensus

Closure (psychology, visual perception): the fact that peripheral vision tends to compress vision and to allow completion of details by already stored inner images

Closure (visual arts): the process by which the mind fills in

missing details of a framed object, as in the panels of a comic, or
a cinema/television screen

   Closure (law): an act of closing a public trial
   Poetic closure
   Transitive closure
   A packaging "closure" is a bottle cap or screw cap

40.

Deep within my body, the past is still alive. Everything that has
ever happened keeps happening. I might be meditating, and then,
suddenly, instead of sitting cross-legged on my bedroom floor in
Connecticut, I am standing in a New Jersey hospital room, hearing the news that my father has died. While lying still in pigeon
pose, my forehead pressed to the floor, suddenly I am in my car,
driving up our driveway to see Michael standing on our front
porch, phone in hand. His eyes meet mine as I grow closer, and I
know that my mother is gone.

   It's a seductive idea, closure—but I think it's a myth. The poet
Anne Sexton was once asked why she wrote almost exclusively
about dark and difficult subjects: *Pain engraves a deeper memory* was
her response. The quieter and more internal I become, the more
these stories unspool. Prayer, meditation, yoga seem to unleash
the past, rather than to bury it. What good does all this searching do, when so much of what I find is hard to take? Why would
anyone sign up for this? Especially when there are so many ways
around it?

Sometimes I want to run away: have a few drinks, take a sleeping pill, buy those overpriced stiletto heels. Anything to sedate myself—to mute the endless loop of stories. And sometimes I give in, and do exactly that. The clarity is too painful, and I want to forget. The problem is, it doesn't work. Not in the long run. There is no permanent forgetting. Though the world of things is persuasive and distracting, the stories always come back, circled in neon. They are all the more alive for having been hidden.

41.

In the years following my father's death, any time I had an important decision to make I asked myself: What would he have wanted me to do? The question became my ritual, my belief system. I was twenty-three years old, and aware that my father had died disappointed in me. Was I going to be okay? Was I going to pull myself out of my downward spiral? Would I find my way in the world? He had no idea, nor did I. In my early twenties, I had constructed a new identity for myself. I had shed the obedient, good, observant girl I had once been, as if stepping out of my skin and into another. I stopped reading, writing, playing the piano, spending time outdoors, going to shul—all the things that had kept my feet on the ground. I became rail thin, hard-edged, interested only in the surfaces of things. If I sensed a whiff of danger, all the better. I figured that I would skate and skid along that dangerous surface for as long as I could, until I crashed. Until something stopped me—if something ever did.

Well, it was indeed a crash that stopped me. Only it wasn't the crash I had imagined. It wasn't *my* crash. My parents' accident destroyed their lives, and in a devastating bit of symmetry, saved mine. *What would my father want me to do?* Over and over, the question became a beacon in my personal darkness, lighting the way. It seemed I couldn't go wrong, as long as I listened to my dead father. He would have wanted me to leave my older, married sociopath of a boyfriend. So I finally did. He would have wanted me to go back to college. So I did that too. He would have wanted me to take care of my mother—and I tried. Oh, how I tried. There was no getting around the Fifth Commandment, *Honor your father and mother.* Not sometimes. Not depending on their behavior. Not when you happen to feel like it. Honor your father and mother no matter what.

Now—five years after my mother's death—she haunts me. She stands over my shoulder as I write. She is the old lady I see on Broadway, walking with a cane, clutching a Fairway shopping bag. At three o'clock in the morning, if I am startled out of sleep, it is my mother who waits in the darkness. She lives in my hips, and is lodged beneath my solar plexus. *Pain engraves a deeper memory.* The deeper I probe, the more I find parts of her inside me, buried artifacts. Closure is impossible.

Honor your father and mother.

I was unable to honor my mother. I fought her, avoided her, pushed her away. *But I gave you life!* she sometimes screamed in frustration. *You wouldn't exist if it hadn't been for me!* She is my own *samskara*—she lingers within me. She will die only when I take my last breath.

42.

Samskara—latent impression; predisposition; consecration; imprint; innate tendency; innate potence; mold; inborn nature; residual impression; purificatory rite; rite of passage.

1. It is a predisposition from past impressions. It is one of the five aggregates according to Buddhism. They are impressions left in the mind after any experience.

2. It is one of the twelve links in the causal chain of existence, according to Buddhism.

3. It is a rite performed with the help of sacred syllables (mantra) to restore a thing to its original pure state.

4. It is a purificatory rite in connection with an individual's life in Brahmanic Indian society. It includes the sacred thread ceremony, marriage rites, funeral rites, etc.

5. It is one of three kinds: velocity (*vega*), by virtue of which an object possesses motion; feeling (*bhavana*), by virtue of which there is memory or recognition; and oscillation (*sthitisthapa-katva*), by means of which a substance returns from a distance to its original position.

43.

If *God doesn't give us more than we can handle* is my least favorite bromide, my second least favorite is this: *Everything happens for a reason.*

On the cover of *People*, the sole survivor of a plane crash expresses his gratitude to God. He doesn't understand why he alone was saved. "I put myself in God's hands," he says. "I have faith that everything happens for a reason." We look for reasons in retrospect. We tell ourselves stories. Every near miss has a narrative. Since the time of the cave dwellers we have attempted to take the random events of our existence and fashion them into something that makes sense.

Shortly after we moved to Connecticut, I got a call one morning from the concierge at the inn down the road. A guest at the inn had seen my books in the gift shop, and asked if I lived nearby. He wondered if I might be able to meet with him. I admit, I was curious. It's not every day that I get a call like that, out of the blue. What did this guy want? Was he a fan? A stalker? If so, he was a well-heeled stalker. The inn is no quiet country B&B. A late de Kooning hangs in the state-of-the-art spa, its yellow and blue swirls the only color in a room filled with white sofas and chaises draped with white cashmere blankets. The effect is of a heavenly sanitarium, *Magic Mountain* complete with haute-lite cuisine and a lavender-scented steam bath.

The man and his wife greeted me in the lobby.

"I'll leave you two," said the wife. She was a lovely woman, perhaps fifteen years older than me. She was wrapped in a bathrobe, her hair slick with massage oil. "He has a lot to talk to you about."

I followed the man into the great room. He was quite tall, distinguished even in his weekend casual clothes, gray-haired and wearing wire-rimmed glasses. As we poured ourselves some ginger tea and settled on the sofa beneath the de Kooning, I wondered. Did he know me, somehow? A friend of my family? He had a way about him—a certain kindness in his face—that reminded me of my father. I guessed he was in his mid-sixties.

"I loved *Slow Motion*," he said. "It meant a lot to me."

Slow Motion is very much a young woman's story—a memoir of the mess I made of my coming-of-age. Why would it speak to him?

A spa attendant whisked away the saucer on which we had placed our used tea bags. There was an absolute absence of clutter. Even the garbage cans were empty. I had recently taught a memoir workshop at the spa, to several women who had come to this most privileged place with some very heavy baggage: one whose Silicon Valley billionaire husband had left her; another whose only daughter had committed suicide.

The man reached for his cup of tea, then set it down without taking a sip. "I was the last person who got on the last elevator to leave Windows on the World before the plane hit," he said. "Someone held the door open for me. I don't know who it was. Later, I remembered things. I remembered the sight of an arm reaching out"—here his voice cracked—"and holding the door open."

He went on to tell the details: he'd been having breakfast with a woman from an arts organization who had asked a favor he was unable to grant. As they left the restaurant, he stopped at a few tables to greet acquaintances. Once in the elevator, he rode all the way down to the lobby with his breakfast companion instead of getting off on the seventy-eighth floor to go to his office—his life saved not once but twice, based on timing and split-second choices.

He shrugged. It looked almost involuntary, like a spasm. "Trying to be a nice guy, I guess."

He looked at me, this man with the kind face who reminded me of my father. His eyes, behind his glasses, were filled with the bottomless pain of his own good fortune. All around us, men and women padded by in thick white robes and plastic flip-flops.

"I keep thinking there has to be a reason," said the man. "Something I'm supposed to do now. Only I don't know what it is."

I was certain that there was no reason. No reason at all. There was only this: luck, timing, consequences. Infinitesimal moments that added up and became personal tragedies, personal miracles. God wasn't up in the sky pulling the strings. There was only one thing to say—one thing I understood from my own life, my own personal tragedy. Finally, I understood why this man had responded to *Slow Motion*. My parents' accident wasn't an event that changed the world, but it had changed me. I had risen out of the ashes of that sadness and loss, and did the only thing worth doing. I had tried to become a better person.

"You *make* it mean something. That's all you can do."

44.

I've been having trouble maintaining a sense of solitude. Oh, sure, I have the hours during the day when Jacob is at school, Michael is at his office, the dogs are asleep on the kitchen floor. But solitude—the kind of silence inside of which one can *transact some private business with the fewest obstacles*, in Thoreau's words—does not simply have to do with being alone.

I can be frenetically alone. I can be anxiously alone. I can be alone with ten thousand thoughts racing through my head. These kinds of states aren't productive; they don't count. The kind of solitude I long for is what I was able to achieve during those days at Kripalu, when my mind felt ironed clean. All it took was yoga and meditation around the clock! But I don't live at Kripalu—and if I did, I imagine that the magic I felt there would slowly evaporate. The thing is this: I know I can find it right here at home, though certainly it's more of a struggle and requires greater discipline. I have found it on my yoga mat. I have found it during meditation. I have found it when, first thing in the morning, instead of checking my e-mail (*Free shipping from Land's End! Twenty-four-hour J. Crew sale!*) I open Virginia Woolf's *A Writer's Diary* to a random page. This morning's entry: "Arrange the pieces as they come." Is there any other way to live than arranging the pieces as they come?

So if I know all this, why such resistance? The door is always open. Why not go through? Why does it seem that I require friction, a certain amount of agony, before I batter the door down like a blind and crazy ram? Yesterday I wrote to Steve Cope that I am alternately as good as I've ever been, and full of despair. His response: "The tension arc between despair and wonderful is very good for the writing, don't you think?"

45.

On the morning my father died, his younger brother—my uncle Harvey—arrived by taxi from New York. He found me in the hospital corridor outside my mother's room, making calls.

"Who's with Paul?" Harvey asked. He was breathless, his grief wild and angry, leaving no room for my own. I had never been close to Harvey, but still, I wanted to collapse into him. I wanted him to recognize that I was still practically a kid. *I don't know how to do this,* I felt like saying.

"I asked the doctors to leave him in his room," I said. "Until we—"

"No one's watching him?" Harvey wheeled around and raced back down the corridor to the elevator bank. My father's room was in another unit, two floors up. I hadn't been aware of the sacred tradition of *shmira,* in which the body is not left alone—not even for a single second—between the moment of death and the moment of burial. Later that afternoon, my uncle would inform me—in an accusatory tone, as if I should have known better—that my father had been intubated, that a tracheotomy had been performed in a last-ditch effort to save him, and that the various tubes and equipment had been left in his body in a way not consistent with Jewish law.

You fucked up, was the subtext. *And you can't fix it now.*

My mother was fighting for her life. Given the scope of her own injuries, she wasn't expected to survive the shock of this—the loss of her husband. Sedated, on painkillers, she drifted in and out of consciousness as the Shapiro family descended—an Orthodox SWAT team. There were precise, choreographed steps to take: the appropriate funeral home to be contacted; the paid death notice announcing the location of shivah; the summoning of the *chevre kadisha,* a holy society consisting of Jews who cleanse and purify the body, and recite the required psalms and prayers asking God to forgive all sins and grant eternal peace to the deceased.

Riverside, I heard through the thick, cottony wall of my own grief. *Shivah at Gram's*. Wait a minute. Riverside Chapel was in Manhattan. As was my grandmother's apartment. I looked at my mother, her shattered legs scissored in traction. Her face still lacerated, black and blue. She looked frail in her bed, surrounded by my father's family—a group of people with whom she had barely been on speaking terms for most of the twenty-eight years of her marriage. She stared at the ceiling as they discussed different rabbis. Names—Shlomo Riskin, Isaac Swift—were floated. Plans seemed to be happening all around my mother, but they did not include her. And then, as if issuing a news bulletin from a faraway land, my mother spoke:

"The service will be here in the hospital," she said. "I'm going to attend my own husband's funeral."

The next morning, my mother was transferred from her bed to a stretcher, then wheeled through the hospital's main lobby, past the gift shop and into the auditorium for my father's funeral. Her cardiologist, internist, and trauma specialist were all nearby. *Don't die, don't die, don't die* was my mantra, the ceaseless whisper in my head. Any horror seemed possible—no, more than possible. Likely.

I held my mother's hand and stood next to her stretcher. The service was about to begin. The auditorium was filled to capacity: Wall Street bankers in business suits, neighbors I remembered from years of backyard barbecues and pool parties, my mother's tennis buddies. The previous night, my mother had asked her own brother, a college professor, to speak at the funeral. Not Harvey. She had also asked a senior partner at my father's firm to speak.

Not some famous rabbi. At this modern funeral service orchestrated by my mother from her hospital bed, my father's family had no role. They clustered together in the front row, their dark coats and prayer books setting them apart.

After the service, a line of black cars idled near the hospital's main entrance. Of course, my mother couldn't make the trip—not even by ambulance. I had to leave her behind to go bury my father. I watched my cousin Henry, Shirley's younger son, climb into the hearse, siddur in hand. He davened the whole time. He wore a fedora and a dark overcoat; a muffler covered the lower part of his face. Henry, a member of the *chevre kadisha*, had stayed with my father the night before. I kept my eyes trained on the hearse as we snaked down the leafy suburban streets near the hospital. I was afraid of losing sight of my father as we sped along the wide New Jersey highways of my childhood, crossed over into lower Manhattan, then made our way through downtown traffic to the Brooklyn Battery Tunnel. Finally we emerged at a massive, old cemetery in Bensonhurst where my grandfather and great-grandparents were buried.

I had never been to the Shapiro family plot. I had, in fact, never been to a funeral of any kind. The only ideas I had about funerals came from the movies—and this wasn't anything like that. *From dust thou art, and unto dust shalt thou return.* An Orthodox burial takes these words from Genesis seriously. The body, as prepared and purified by the *chevre kadisha*, is wrapped in a white shroud and placed in a plain pine box. No Astroturf covers the earth around the burial site. Cremation is considered abhorrent. Embalming is expressly forbidden. Viewing, flowers, incense are discouraged. In the starkest possible manner, the dead are returned to the earth.

My legs were unsteady as I followed the pallbearers—my cousins—through the crumbling paths of the Brooklyn cemetery. The el train rattled overhead. Somewhere, a dog was barking. My cousins paused a number of times along the way. I thought they were lost. I didn't realize that the pausing is customary—a sign of reluctance to depart with the dead. I didn't know the prayers, or their meaning. What was happening? My father was inside that flimsy box, and his family was burying him at his own father's feet. In the midst of their sadness and shock, they knew exactly what to do. Here, *I* was out of place. An interloper.

Mordechai sang "El Malei Rachamim." My cousins lowered their uncle by long straps into the ground. Someone handed me a shovel and pointed.

I lifted a shovelful of dirt and spilled it onto my father's casket. My half sister did the same. Then Shirley, Harvey, their grown children. The men shuffled. Their voices rose and fell; now a murmur, now a wail. They were schooled in this ritual, and the very fact of it gave them a kind of solace. The washing, the wrapping, the standing guard, the praying. After my father's coffin was no longer visible, the small crowd formed two parallel columns, as if in a square dance. The immediate family was meant to walk through. As we did, the prescribed condolence was offered: *Hamakom y'nachem etkhem b'tokh sh'ar aveilei Tzion v'Yrushalayim.* May God comfort you among all the mourners of Zion and Jerusalem. I felt no such comfort, but I did know one thing: this funeral was precisely what my father would have wanted.

46.

Writers often say that the hardest part of writing isn't the writing itself; it's the sitting down to write. The same is true of yoga, meditation, and prayer. The sitting down, the making space. The *doing*. It sounds so simple, doesn't it? Unroll the mat. Sit cross-legged on the floor. *Just do it.* Close your eyes and express a silent need, a wish, a moment of gratitude. What's so hard about that? Except—it is hard. The usual distractions—the clutter and piles of life—are suddenly, unusually enticing. The worst of it, I've come to realize, is that the thing that stops me—the shadow that casts a cold darkness across the best of my intentions—isn't the puppy, the e-mail, the UPS truck, the school conference, the phone, the laundry, the to-do lists. It's *me* that stops me. *Things get stuck*, the osteopath once said with a shrug. He gestured to the area where the neck meets the head. The place where the body ends and the mind begins. *Things get stuck.* It sounded so simple when he said it. It's me, and the things that are stuck. Standing in my way.

47.

We don't get a lot of unexpected visitors. Our driveway is a quarter of a mile long, and cars don't turn into it accidentally. Every once in a while, though, an unfamiliar vehicle pulls up to the house. If I'm home alone, I tend to get a little nervous. I hold the phone in one hand, ready to call 911 as I peer out the window.

Recently, a car full of young men dressed in black suits and white shirts drove up to the house on a Sunday morning. They didn't look like ax murderers. An older woman wearing a tweed skirt and Shetland sweater was with them; she was the one who knocked on our front door.

"Michael! It's the Seventh Day Adventists!" I yelled. I didn't like dealing with proselytizers. I never knew what to say. *We're all set. No thanks—really.*

Michael walked outside, the puppy at his heels. He actually liked engaging these people. I watched through the window as he chatted with the woman. What could they possibly be discussing? She handed him some sort of pamphlet, then waved good-bye.

"We talked about the dog," Michael said when he came back in. "She didn't want to talk about religion. She wanted to give me this. Oh, and they weren't Seventh Day Adventists."

"Well, what were they?"

"I'm not sure. Witnesses, I think."

Michael had only taken the pamphlet to be polite. He tossed it into the recycling bin. I fished it out. The pamphlet was titled *Would You Like to Know the Truth?* Inside was a list of questions:

Does God Really Care About Us?
Will War and Suffering Ever End?
What Happens to Us When We Die?
Is There Any Hope for the Dead?
How Can I Pray and Be Heard by God?
How Can I Find Happiness in Life?

I definitely wanted to know the truth. I glanced through the pamphlet, which also contained photographs: a bandaged child, a graveyard, a woman clutching a prayer book to her chest. *How can I pray and be heard by God?* This question in particular interested me. According to the pamphlet, the Bible—this would be the New Testament—teaches that we must not say the same things over and over again in our prayers. If we want God to listen, we must pray in the way that he approves. To do that, we need to learn what God's will is and then pray accordingly.

The pamphlet cited Matthew 6:7, which I promptly looked up. After all, I was an equal-opportunity seeker of wisdom. What did I care where it came from? *And when you pray, you shall not be like the hypocrites. For they love to stand praying in synagogues* (ouch!) *and on the corners of the streets, so that they may be seen by men. Assuredly, I say to you, they have their reward.* (Double ouch!) *But you, when you pray, go into your room, and when you have shut the door, pray to your Father, who is in the secret place; and your Father who sees in secret will reward you openly.*

I liked the idea of prayer as something private and fluid. I thought of the High Holiday services of my youth. The ladies in their new outfits, the men squirming uncomfortably. The children playing outside as the adults did their duty. Then I thought about my own yoga practice, and the way, sometimes, the phrase from that old Dunkin' Donuts commercial would pop into my head as I began my routine sun salutations: Time to make the donuts, I would think as I bent forward, then jumped back. Time to make the donuts.

But maybe there was good reason for the routine—for repeating the same gestures, the same words, again and again. As my father wrapped his tefillin around and around his arm, the familiar action was a meditative one, a preparation for prayer. Could he have gotten there without it? When I unroll my yoga mat and place my hands in *namaste*, I may be making the donuts, but I am also performing a ritual that allows me to enter a contemplative place—a place in which I might come upon something wordless and profound. Maybe the rituals are a doorway to prayer. But I spent most of my life confusing them with prayer itself.

48.

I didn't know how to pray. I knew the Hebrew words and melodies of my childhood—I could recite the entire siddur by heart—but I didn't know what any of it meant. Despite my yeshiva education, the language was elusive to me. Oh, I could pick up a few words here and there. *Melech* meant "king." *Olam* meant "world." But basically, it was gone. How could I have gone from fluent to nothing? Perhaps Hebrew itself was a *samskara*. Perhaps one day, while in a deep yoga pose, it would all come flooding back.

But honestly, I was glad I no longer understood. Even in English translation, the prayers themselves disturbed me. I didn't want to plead with God, or bargain with him, or flatter him. I wanted to access him. To find a way to speak to him without feeling ridiculous. When I was in shul, I sang, and the singing itself stirred something within me: memory, intense longing. If nothing else, it was a deep connection to the past. But it didn't feel like prayer—or at least, what I hoped prayer might feel like.

Each day, I kept making the donuts. It wasn't simply the yoga practice, the attempts to meditate, the reading and thinking and enforced daily solitude. By doing each of these things, I was creating an environment, I hoped, in which I might continue to explore and deepen my perception. "The great spirits of religious traditions do not solve all questions but live *in* the questions, and return to them again and again, not as a circle returns, but as an ascending spiral comes to the same place, each time at a higher level," writes Rabbi David Wolpe. Each day, when I unrolled my mat, opened a book, let the phone ring, sat still instead of jumping up and reacting to whatever was going on in my mind, I was attempting exactly that: a return to the questions.

Some days were harder than others. At times, I was convinced that I had made a huge mistake, delving this intensely into spiritual matters. Was I becoming one of those earnest, humorless people? Who did I think I was, anyway? I was a *novelist*. If I was good at anything, it was at making things up. Writing fiction—following the line of words, as Annie Dillard once put it—was the closest thing I had ever known to an act of faith. I kept moving in small steps, both forward and back. With each step, I had no certainty that there would be ground beneath me.

But on rare occasions, I felt something else. Something different. It was a sense, not of presence, but of oneness. There was no difference between *me* and *it*—nothing separating me from the invisible fabric that made up everything around me. When this happened, it did not feel revelatory. There were no violins, no exploding lights. There was nothing epiphanic, orgiastic, ecstatic, about it. It was a very quiet sense of *knowing*. The words accompanying this knowledge did not strike me as ridiculous. They did not strike me as anything at all, but rather, emerged from a place beyond self-consciousness. *Please allow my heart to open to all that is.*

49.

In Connecticut, on our hilltop, life was quiet. Gone were the city sounds: the sirens, hisses, street fights, car alarms, the teeming, throbbing, ceaseless pulse of life. Our pace slowed. A different kind of pulse surrounded us now. I noticed the reddish hue of bare tree branches as they began to bud; the silvery frost at dawn. Baby chipmunks darted into the cracks under our front steps. We were surrounded by crickets, field mice, bats, hawks, frogs from the pond across the way. A gray fox roamed our meadow. There were reports of a bear. At night, coyotes howled in the distance.

Suddenly, there were enough—more than enough!—hours in the day. There was no traffic. It took exactly sixteen minutes to drive Jacob to school. No more, no less, barring the unforeseen event of being stuck behind a tractor pulling hay. It took nine minutes to get to the market, eleven minutes to the little French bakery. The thriving metropolis of Great Barrington, Massachusetts, was precisely an hour, door-to-door. It was quiet, all right. So quiet that we could hear the sound of a truck straining uphill a mile away.

In the silence, something shifted. I had left a certain kind of anxiety behind, back in the city. The urban life I had loved for so long—the constant motion, the sense that there was always something exciting happening somewhere—that life had turned on me, once I became a mother. (Or perhaps once my child became so sick. The two events—new motherhood, the near-loss of Jacob—are grafted together in my mind so that it is impossible to think of one without the other.) In the country, I stopped being a person who, in the words of Sylvia Boorstein, *startles easily*. I grew calmer, but beneath that calm was a deep well of loneliness I hadn't known was there. No wonder I had been running as hard and as fast as I could! Anxiety was my fuel. When I stopped, it was all waiting for me: fear, anger, grief, despair, and that terrible, terrible loneliness. What was it about? I was hardly alone. I loved my husband and son. I had great friends, colleagues, students. In the quiet, in the extra hours, I was forced to ask the question, and to listen carefully to the answer: I was lonely for myself.

Who was I, and what did I want for the second half of my life? I mean, I was in the middle of life, the middle of midlife, the middle of a midlife crisis. I had been shaped by choices and decisions, not all of them conscious. I had turned left instead of right; had taken (or not taken) the trip, the flight, the challenge, the chance. Everything I had ever done had led me here—and while here wasn't a bad place at all, it also wasn't enough. Some essential piece of me was missing, and in the quiet of the country I had an opportunity to figure out what, exactly, that missing piece was.

50.

Lacuna (manuscripts): a missing piece of text

    Lacuna (music): an extended silence in a piece of music

    Lacuna (linguistics): a lexical gap in a language

    Lacuna (law): the lack of law or of a legal source addressing a situation

Lacuna (histology): a small space containing an osteocyte in bone

Lacuna (geology): a large gap in the stratigraphic record

Lacunar amnesia (psychology): amnesia about a specific event

Petrovsky lacuna (mathematics): a region where the fundamental solution of a differential equation vanishes

51.

Some of my best conversations with Jacob take place in the car. When the radio is off, the DVD screen tucked away, in the silence the car transforms from a suburban vehicle into a sanctuary. The other day, we were driving home from school, and all of a sudden, Jacob piped up from the back seat: "How do we know we're not dreaming right now?" The idea that we might be dreaming frightened him. He wanted to know what was real. I know he feels great comfort in anything quantifiable: maps, lists, facts, figures. He also thinks a lot about death. *Maybe when we die it feels like dreaming.* Despite evidence to the contrary, he thinks that only very old people die. That life has an expiration date, like his squeezable yogurts. Eighty, he thinks. Or better yet, ninety or one hundred. Comfortably far off for everyone he knows and loves.

Jacob has been coming up with more of these questions lately—perhaps because he has some awareness that I've been thinking about them too. What he doesn't know is that he's the beating heart of my journey. That, had he not been born, I might never have felt this need to explore my intermittent feelings of emptiness and loss. There was always some sort of shiny distraction. Always a way of quieting the voice that exhorted me to think harder, delve deeper. And besides, things were pretty good, particularly when I considered where I had come from; as the poet Jane Kenyon once wrote, "It might have been otherwise."

I had lived most of my adult life thinking that way: *I got out of bed / on two strong legs. / It might have been / otherwise.* But becoming a mother made me greedy. I wanted more than the awareness of my own good fortune—the day, each breath, the quiet, the health of my loved ones, my own two strong legs. I was looking beyond the horizon of my own gratitude—and make no mistake about it, I was grateful. But I knew that past that horizon was a drop, a free fall. There was much that I didn't remember. So much that I had left behind. I couldn't teach my son to be unafraid of his lacunae if I wasn't willing to sit in the deepest hollows of my own.

52.

Is it ever right to give up on a person? To decide—if indeed, it amounts to a decision—that a relationship is beyond hope? What would it take, to arrive at such a place? And, having arrived at such a place, what then? In the Yom Kippur service during the Ashamnu, the ritual recitation of communal sins, among the sins of committing slander, adultery, covetousness, there is this: *for the sin of succumbing to dismay.*

To succumb to dismay. It had never seemed like much of a sin, but it did seem that there might be a high price for succumbing. Shortly after Michael and I decided to move from Brooklyn to Connecticut, he turned to me one afternoon and asked what I was going to do about my mother. It had been a year since I'd seen her. I had stopped speaking to her during Jacob's illness. It was a horrible choice, but not a difficult one: *my mother or my child.*

It shouldn't have surprised me that it had come to this. I had spent years—my whole life, really—trying to make peace with my mother. She was at war with the world, but with no one so much as me. My very existence seemed an affront and disappointment to her. Even as a child, I felt myself shrink in her presence, trying to make myself invisible so that her rage might pass over me. As I grew up, I developed the protective mechanism of forgetting. I forgot the pain she caused me until I felt it again—and again.

When Jacob had become ill, my mother dismissed his illness too. She thought I was exaggerating—that it was no big deal. She screamed that I wasn't paying attention to *her.* She told me I'd better watch out or my marriage would fall apart, because Michael and I seemed depressed. Finally I walked away. I couldn't be Jacob's mother and her daughter at the same time. I had written my mother a note when Jacob seemed to be recovering, and had called her on the morning of the attacks on the World Trade Center. But that had been the extent of our contact. She had called, faxed, e-mailed, FedExed, and otherwise tried to get hold of me. But Jacob's illness had taken me apart and put me back together. My heart had grown tougher, more resilient. Life was too short, I told myself. But I hadn't succumbed—not totally. I still had a glimmer of hope. Maybe things could be different. Maybe later.

But now, later was upon us. We were moving to the country. If I didn't reach out to my mother, it might never happen. She wouldn't know how to find me. She could die without anyone knowing it. She had very few friends—she had alienated most of them. Michael knew that for my own future peace of mind, I needed to be able to tell myself that I had done everything I could. Absolutely everything. *So what are you going to do about your mother?*

The psychiatrist's office was on the ground floor of an apartment building on lower Park Avenue. Like many such offices, it announced itself discreetly, with a small bronze plaque. I had arrived early. I walked east, to Lexington Avenue, in search of a Starbucks—but coffee was the last thing I needed. I was already hopped up. My heart was racing; my fingers tingled. It was a bitter cold day, and the street felt like a wind tunnel. I should have been home in Brooklyn, packing up our brownstone. We were moving in less than a month.

I rounded the corner back to the doctor's office, then checked my watch. It was three o'clock—the appointed time. Just as I was about to buzz the doctor's intercom, a taxi pulled up in front of the building. She emerged slowly, swinging one leg, then the other, to the curb. The full-length fur coat, the freshly highlighted hair, the big, dark sunglasses: she didn't look like a seventy-eight-year-old woman who had once been shattered by a near-fatal car accident. She was regal and beautiful as she greeted me, her cheekbone sharp and cool against my own.

"Hello, my dear daughter," she said.

We walked together into the psychiatrist's office that cold winter day. It was the first of what turned out to be six sessions we attended. We took our seats—she erect in the center of a sofa, me slumped into the farthermost chair. What did I hope for? I know this much: I hoped. Fervently, deeply, powerfully, I hoped that in the presence of a neutral stranger with an advanced degree, my mother and I could connect.

Six sessions—six hours—and there are huge gaps in my memory, lacunae. I do remember the tone of her raised voice. The usual phrases—*How dare you? I was a wonderful mother! You seem to feel the need to turn me into a monster*—and the way they lost their power in the presence of a third party. It wasn't long before he took my side. I hadn't anticipated this. I know they're not supposed to take sides, but he did. *Irene, you're not listening to Dani. Excuse me. Excuse me, Irene. Irene! You're not with us here. You're not understanding anything that's going on. Irene!* Rather than feeling vindicated, I felt guilty. It seemed cruel, and my fault, somehow. My relationship with my mother had always brought into question any sense I had of myself as a good and decent person. Surely I was poisoning the psychiatrist. *Poison* was a word my mother liked to use a lot.

At what turned out to be our final session, my mother came in carrying an oversize manila envelope. I didn't think much of it at the time, or the way she rested it next to her on the sofa, or the way her gaze occasionally shifted to it. The psychiatrist was being particularly hard on her that day. *I understand why Dani feels like you don't hear her, Irene. She isn't real to you. You're just talking at her.* Halfway through that last session, my mother jumped to her feet faster than I would have thought possible, and the envelope clattered to the floor. Her face was white with rage as she bent down, gathered it up, and stormed out of the office.

What followed—the next two events—have become forever linked in my mind. My mother called that night with the news that the manila envelope contained the results of a brain scan that showed her to have metastasized cancer. *Didn't you wonder what was in the envelope? Didn't you even care?* When I got off the phone, shaken, I called the psychiatrist. Had he known? Had she told him? There was a long silence, during which I realized that he wasn't at liberty to say. But he did offer me this, his parting words: *In thirty years of practice, I have never said this to a patient, but there is no hope for you and your mother. None at all.*

53.

A small group of people gathers together at my friend Abby's Manhattan apartment once a month to study Torah with Burt Visotzky, a respected and gifted rabbi. When she first invited me to join the group, I felt conflicted. I had spent my childhood confused by Torah—learning by rote, understanding nothing. But I went anyway, and now I look forward to these Tuesday evenings—in part because of the feeling that each person in that room is engaged in a personal struggle with faith. Before we begin discussing the Torah portion, we go around in a circle and everyone says a few words about how they're doing. This never fails to make me a little nervous. It reminds me of AA, except that most of us are drinking wine.

Last week, I was fresh from my second visit to Kripalu—another yoga and meditation retreat—when I went to Torah study. When it came my turn to speak, I was raw, vulnerable. I had just spent several days with a heightened awareness of what was going on in my mind, and it wasn't pretty. I talked about how hard I was finding it to meditate. In almost every meditation instruction, the phrase *begin again* emerges as a theme. Your mind is wandering? Begin again. Clouded over with thoughts? Begin again. A twinge in your knee? Don't judge it, or beat yourself up about it. Let it go. Return to the breath. Begin again.

Well, I was having a hard time beginning again, and I was judging myself for it. Instead of gently, with compassion, returning to the breath, I was caught in a cycle of self-recrimination. What was going on inside my head was so stupid! So shallow and ridiculous! My mind was consumed either with the past or the future. I became lost in conversations that hadn't happened and probably never would. I had been practicing yoga for many years, had developed this meditation practice, had begun to explore my Jewish roots with a semi-open mind—but still, there was all this internal chatter. I couldn't seem to quiet it. Why couldn't I remain in the present for longer than, oh, say, three seconds? I had a new understanding of the word *scatterbrained*.

The people in the group were nodding and looked sympathetic, but when I finished speaking I felt even worse. Why had I even talked about my struggles with meditation in this Torah study group? One thing had nothing to do with the other. As we turned to the text, I felt exposed by the hours and hours of looking inward. What was the point of any of this? How did it all connect—if it connected at all? The yoga, meditation, reading, Torah study—it felt futile. The words swam together. I sank into my chair and tried to disappear.

I wasn't the only frustrated person in the room that night. Burt read aloud from Genesis 30, in which two sisters, Rachel and Leah, use surrogate handmaidens to compete for the status of having produced the most children for Jacob. This prompted one woman in the group to ask why we read these stories. What are we supposed to get out of them? I had often wondered the same thing. "I mean," she said, "these people do terrible things to each other." Burt smiled in agreement. It was true—there was no question, really—that these biblical characters were not exactly exemplars of ethical behavior. But there was something more. I had become friends with Burt over these many months, and could feel the intensity of what he was about to say before he even said it. "Because they're ours to grapple with. Their human frailties allow us to see our own. We doubt and question them, generation after generation. It's our text."

On the long ride back to Connecticut, Michael driving, I kept thinking about the whole idea of human frailty, and how—paradoxically—the recognition of frailty contained within it a kind of strength. What Burt had said had struck a nerve: the questioning was the true work of engagement. To question, to doubt, to rail against, even to reject—these were our prerogative. As a child, I had been taught not to question. But as Paul Tillich once wrote, doubt isn't the opposite of faith; it's an element of faith. If only I could hold close to that idea. If only I could gently, simply—like a child learning to walk—begin again, and again, and again, whether returning to the Torah, to the meditation cushion, or simply to myself.

As we sped along the highway, I checked my e-mail. There was a message from Burt: *I want to quote you a Mishnah text from tractate*

Berakhot about prayer: "The early pious ones used to meditate for an hour before praying." I know it feels to you like you are starting over each time, but really all you are doing is bringing your footsteps back to our well-trod path. That's not starting over. It's picking up the thread.

54.

Michael and I were out to dinner with another couple—very good friends of ours. The husband was someone I've known since seventh grade. With my parents gone and few relatives left, these ties to my past have become increasingly important to me. This guy was at my bat mitzvah! He saw me wearing that dorky peach corduroy suit and my first pair of heels! I knew him when he was a shrimpy, late-blooming adolescent, as opposed to the well-known actor he later became. We were familiar with each other's high school crushes and embarrassments.

Dinner was at a Manhattan restaurant, a hushed place with artfully arranged food and flattering lighting. We were grown-ups now—there was no doubt about that. At least we looked like grown-ups, had grown-up lives. Maybe even acted like grown-ups. He had two young children, I had one. We'd both been a bit beaten up by life but were, at the moment, weathering things pretty well. The four of us were talking about our kids when the subject turned to memory. Why do we remember the particular things we do? Great pain certainly carves its own neurological path. But why random, ordinary moments?

"I remember sitting on the kitchen counter, watching my

mother boil me an egg," my friend said. He looked puzzled, reaching back. "She must have made me eggs hundreds of times. But I remember that one particular time."

I knew what all of us were thinking. What would our children remember? The oldest among them—Jacob—was nine. What ordinary moments had imprinted themselves on him at this point? And what painful ones? Michael and I rarely fought, but there had been a fight or two over the years that Jacob had witnessed. Would that be what he took away from our peaceful, happy family life? His parents red-faced and screaming at each other? I hoped not. God, I hoped not. But who knew?

I tried to create a daily sense of constancy and ritual: family dinners, holiday traditions. On Hanukkah, we lit the menorah each year with Jacob's best friends. We ordered bagels and lox from Barney Greengrass on the Upper West Side for Yom Kippur, and had a crowd to break the fast. On our kitchen table, I kept a book of Buddhist wisdom, open to a different page each day. Most days, we remembered to read the little snippet of wisdom and look at the accompanying photograph. The black-necked cranes of Bhutan. The monk meditating in the hidden valley, his face rapt and peaceful. Had any of it seeped in? Would Jacob be sitting in a restaurant with friends some day when he was old enough to need bifocals to study the wine list, and remember some random thing from his childhood?

My mother yelled at me because I couldn't find my socks.

My dad made me bacon.

Who the hell knew? It was all in there, conscious or unconscious. What rose to the surface—and why?

"I feel no connection to the kid I was," Michael suddenly said.

I had never heard him say anything like this before. "I'm a completely different person."

"Me too," said our friend.

I understood feeling like a completely different person. I had been a late bloomer too, and when I thought back to my teenage self, my twenty-something self, I had a hard time understanding how I had gotten from *there* to *here*. But no connection? I looked at my friend across the table. I could still see the seventh grader I had once known, alive inside him. Could he see that in me? Was there—surely there must be—a through line connecting the disparate parts of ourselves? I had very few memories of my childhood, and my adolescence is a blur. My life came into focus for me around the time my father died. But still, I knew that each part of me—the lost adolescent girl, the rebellious, miserable young woman, the confused, grief-stricken daughter, the grown woman still trying to sort it all out—is linked one to the next, like a fragile chain of paper dolls.

Nope, no connection. Completely different person. I could see that it would be desirable, maybe even preferable, to disavow pieces of the past—all the uncomfortable, unexplainable, embarrassing bits. But I knew better. I had experienced my own memory as a living thing, a palpable presence in my body. I had felt my past unfurl inside me as if it had a mind of its own. These layers of ourselves are always there, waiting for the right moment to emerge. The cooking of an egg. An overheard argument. A walk in the woods. The black-necked cranes of Bhutan. A jumble, perhaps, but nothing is ever missing. Just hidden from view.

55.

I kept coming across the term *householder.* In Buddhist readings and teachings, it cropped up again and again. *Householder.* Loosely translated from the Pali, it meant "layperson." That was me. I was a layperson. I had a home and a family, and was very attached to both. I had no intention of renouncing home life. With any luck, I would never become a wandering ascetic. So what did this mean, to be a householder? Was it possible to do anything more than skim the surface? And if not, was skimming the surface better than nothing at all?

Householder was defined narrowly as a wealthy and presti- gious family patriarch: a guild foreman, banker, or merchant. But Buddha had specific advice for women householders as well:

Be capable at one's work.

Work with diligence and skill.

Manage domestic help skillfully (if relevant) and treat them fairly.

Perform household duties efficiently.

Be hospitable to one's husband's parents and friends.

Be faithful to one's husband; protect and invest family earnings.

Discharge responsibilities lovingly and conscientiously.

Accomplish faith.

Practice generosity.

Cultivate wisdom.

56.

Accomplish faith. There was a time in my life I would have scoffed at the notion, but now it seemed to me that faith really is an accomplishment. If accomplishment is, in part, defined as something requiring effort, certainly I was learning that faith required enormous effort.

My various rituals—the yoga, meditation, thinking, reading, Torah study—these were disciplines. They had become, to some degree, habit. But it was in the space around these rituals that faith resided. It was in the emptiness, the pause between actions, the stillness when one thing was finished but the next had not yet begun. Paradoxically, this was where effort came in, because it was so hard to be empty. To pause. To be still—not leaning forward, not falling back. Steady in the present—not even waiting. Just being. Could I just drive the car? Just cook dinner? Just walk the dogs in the front meadow and take in the rustling trees, the chirping critters in the distance? Why was it so difficult? So scary? Why did something that should be effortless require so much effort?

Every once in a while I would touch upon this state of emptiness. I would feel it for a second or two, perhaps three. And then I would quickly pull myself back, as if from an abyss. The Buddhist teacher Jack Kornfield once asked an audience whether it's possible to stop—let ourselves be a little emptier, a little more silent, more in touch with the spaces between words. The key word was *between.* When I allowed myself to fearlessly enter that between-place even for a few seconds, I accomplished faith.

57.

Life was very different in Connecticut. Though we were only a two-hour drive from the city, it might as well have been a five-hour flight. Friends occasionally came to visit, and I could practically see the thought bubbles escaping from their heads as they walked from their car to our front porch. *Do they have neighbors? Does Jacob have anyone to play with? Where do they buy food?* It wasn't nearly as isolated as that, though in fact we didn't know the people on our street. I saw them nearly every day through the windshield of my car, but this was the country, not the suburbs. No one greeted us with a homemade apple pie when we moved in. People tended to keep to themselves. I did have nicknames for my neighbors: the lady jogging; the couple walking; the one who doesn't wave. In lieu of facts, I invented stories. The lady jogging was a recent widow who dealt with her grief by running; the couple walking was doing so on doctor's orders for the sake of the husband's health; the one who doesn't wave was the grown daughter of a war criminal.

Jacob began preschool when we settled in, at a small school about fifteen minutes from our house. Each morning I drove past grazing cows, along a rutted dirt road, then pulled into the parking lot. I held Jacob's hand as we walked through the glass doors into school, hugged him good-bye at his classroom door like every other parent in the place. Once he was settled in his classroom, I tried—this is the only word for it—I tried to escape.

Unlike many of the other moms, I didn't want to hang out at Jacob's school. I didn't want to avail myself of the volunteering opportunities: the book fair, the auction. You couldn't have paid me to stay for the Tuesday-morning Pilates class in the gymnasium downstairs. I was confused by my own response to the school community. Didn't I want to be part of a community? Didn't I love my child and want the best for him? Of course I did—so why was I making the quick dash back to my car, keeping my head down, avoiding eye contact? As I ducked past the other moms congregated in small groups, I felt isolated, though of course I was responsible for my own isolation.

Certainly I was still shivering in the shadow of Jacob's illness. It was so rare, there were so few good outcomes—I had trouble trusting that it was really over. I had read stories on the Internet about relapses. I held my breath, waiting, girding myself, preparing for the worst, always thinking *what if.*

What if he has a seizure?

What if I let my guard down?

What if something goes wrong?

We had left New York, yes—but we had brought the past with us. Motherhood was still new for me—and I had barely known it without stomach-lurching fear. As I surreptitiously watched the moms, I envied their innocence. One of them told me that she had given birth to her youngest in the local hospital, and it was exactly like a hotel. "They bring you a smoothie afterward," she said. But that hospital doesn't even have a NICU, I thought. What if there had been an emergency?

I had begun to feel—and it was a bitter feeling—that the world could be divided into two kinds of people: those with an awareness of life's inherent fragility and randomness, and those who believed they were exempt. Parenthood had created an even wider gulf between these two categories. I was firmly on the shore of fragility and randomness, and I could barely make out the exempt people dancing across the way. They seemed like a different species to me. Honestly, I resented them. They were having such a good time.

I didn't know that there was a third way of being. Life was unpredictable, yes. A speeding car, a slip on the ice, a ringing phone, and suddenly everything changes forever. To deny that is to deny life—but to be consumed by it is also to deny life. The third way—inaccessible to me as I slunk down the halls—had to do with holding this paradox lightly in one's own hands. To think: It is true, the speeding car, the slip on the ice, the ringing phone. It is true, and yet here I am listening to my boy sing as we walk down the corridor. Here I am giving him a hug. Here we are—together in this, our only moment.

58.

My mother's mother—the only grandparent I ever really knew—spoke in Yiddish expressions that were variations on the same theme:

Alevei, she used to say whenever it seemed something really good might happen. This meant, *It should only happen.* It also somehow implied that it probably wouldn't. *Kayn ayn hora*, she'd say. *There should be no evil eye.* It seemed the evil eye—a curse—was always in the process of being warded off, and the way to ward it off was to be aware of it. Plans were never made without a caveat. See you next week? *God willing.* You'll come for Passover? *I should live and be well.*

As a child, I used to secretly make fun of my grandmother for all of her quaint expressions, but increasingly I found them creeping into my own vocabulary. *God willing.* The words themselves connote a God who's actually keeping tabs on things—but maybe the meaning behind the words is this: the awareness, simply, of life's unpredictability.

It was another Jewish grandmother, Sylvia Boorstein, who pointed out to me that these translated Yiddish phrases are in the hortatory subjunctive, an unusual tense that is used in the Buddhist *metta* phrases: *May I be protected and safe; may I be contented and pleased.* Not so different, really, from *I should live and be well.* The Old Testament also makes good use of the hortatory subjunctive: *Let us come forward to the Holy of Holies with a true heart in full assurance of faith.* These are statements that command oneself and one's associates to join in some action—a communal urging.

I was back on my cushion, along with one hundred and fifty other people, once again listening to Sylvia. She was conducting a three-day silent retreat at the Garrison Institute, a former monastery perched on a cliff overlooking the Hudson River. I had signed up for the retreat impulsively, after seeing a notice about it on Sylvia's Web site. I didn't think too hard about what a silent retreat might mean. I figured it would be okay. Sylvia and I had become friends over the months since we'd first met at Kripalu.

We'd read each other's books, e-mailed back and forth, met for a long breakfast during one of her visits to New York from northern California. I felt a profound safety in her presence—the safety of being seen and known.

But here it was the first night of the retreat, and I was jittery. Would I be able to sleep in my little monk's cell? The bed didn't look very comfortable. What about the communal bathrooms? I hadn't shared a bathroom with a group of strangers since college. Was there coffee in the morning? And what about the silence? No talking at all? Not good morning, hello, excuse me, thank you? What about texting? iChat? Was there Wi-Fi at the monastery?

"The mind ties itself into gratuitous knots, as a result of habit," Sylvia was saying. Gratuitous knots were exactly what I was experiencing. One thought connecting to another, twisting around and around, becoming impossibly tangled. I looked at my tiny, gray-haired friend. She had been forty—and a mother of four—when she discovered Buddhism. Now, at seventy-three, she had a deep well of wisdom, compassion, and equanimity to draw from. I wasn't much for auras, but I swear I could see her glow.

As we prepared to meditate on the navy blue *zafu*s and *zabuton*s laid out neatly in rows, I felt myself beginning to panic. I was reminded of the way Sylvia had described her own mind when she was first practicing: *A mind with a lot of energy scanning the horizon for what to worry about.* Who was I without my worry? How would it be—was it even possible?—to let go of the incessant fretting? I was so used to the noise in my head that I wasn't sure if I even existed without it. Attempting daily meditation for twenty minutes in the privacy of my bedroom was one thing. Seventy-two hours of communal silence was quite another.

I closed my eyes. Sylvia was coteaching with the eminent Buddhist Sharon Salzberg, who had been Sylvia's own teacher many years before. Sharon had gone to India in the early 1970s as a very young woman, and was one of a small core group responsible for bringing meditation to the West. Sharon gave us clear instruction: "Follow the breath in, follow it back out. If your mind wanders, bring it back." My mind wandered almost instantly to the question of why that original core group of young American Buddhists consisted entirely of Jews. I ticked them off in my mind: Joseph Goldstein, Jack Kornfield, Stephen Levine, Sharon Salzberg, Mark Epstein—practically a minyan! Then I caught myself. My ankle throbbed. It was easier to think than to be.

Someone coughed. People shifted on their cushions. Creaking, sneezing, rustling, sniffling. There were endless distractions, inside and out. I thought of something Sharon had said earlier that evening: "The magic moment in the practice is the awareness that our attention has drifted and we've become distracted—and we begin again." I must have come back to my breath dozens of times before the sound of the gong echoed throughout the hall. I was no different from our new puppy back home, who constantly lost track of his red ball, then looked around, sniffing the sky: *Where'd it go? Oh, look over there! What a great twig!*

It was nine o'clock—the end of the first session. One hundred and fifty of us shuffled to our feet. The woman in front of me bowed to the golden Buddha seated on his altar. People avoided eye contact. Down the hall and up the stairs we drifted—slowly, dreamily, deliberately. Doors opened and closed. The sound of running water. In the women's bathroom, strangers brushed teeth side by side.

I walked into my room, changed into a robe and slippers. Everything around me felt foreign and unnerving. I reminded myself that I had willingly signed up for this. I was here to retreat into myself—to see the patterns emerging in my own mind. When Sylvia was my age, she regularly went on month-long retreats. She left her family, went to India. She arose each morning at four to meditate. Her wisdom had not been handed to her on a silver platter. What did I expect? Why should spiritual wakefulness be easy?

I climbed into my little bed and turned off the light. It was early. I was wide awake. Back home, Michael and Jacob were probably watching television. I wondered how Jacob's day had been at school. And Michael was waiting for news about whether or not he had gotten a big screenwriting job. Maybe he had heard? Jacob's school reading project was due on Monday. Would Michael remember to help him with it? How were the dogs? I felt selfish, I realized. Selfish and guilty for being away.

On the wooden desk a few feet from my bed, the green light on my computer glowed. *Connect, connect!* The pull of the outside world was irresistible. I turned on my iChat and saw that Michael was online. With a few magic keystrokes, my husband's face filled my computer screen. He was sitting at his desk, in his office at home. I put on my earphones, so I wouldn't disturb anyone. Even the sound of my fingers clicking against the keyboard seemed loud. He waved. I waved back.

Hi, I wrote.

"Hi," he said. "Can you talk?"

No talking. Everything okay?

"The puppy drank out of the toilet and peed on the floor."

Sorry. How's Jacob?

"He's good. I don't know how we're going to get this reading project done, though. It's a logistical nightmare."

Things fall apart when I go away.

"No, they don't."

They do. Things fall apart when I go away.

"No, honey. No, they really don't."

Maybe I should come home.

"Hi, Mommy!"

Jacob heard his father talking to me, and joined him on the screen. Even the dogs got in the picture. They were home, cozy and safe. I was so happy to see them—all of them. And at the same time, I remembered something Sylvia had said during her talk: "My ability to be present in the world with an open heart depends on my ability to be present to myself with an open heart."

"Mommy, why aren't you talking?"

I'm supposed to be silent, sweetie.

"That's weird."

Jacob was right. It was weird. I was writing to my family on a computer while they talked to me through headphones, in a tiny room in a former monastery on the Hudson River, where I had come to meditate. I was already cheating, sort of. But seeing them fill the screen had reminded me of what I was doing and why I was doing it.

Good night, guys.

"Love you, honey. Don't worry about us. We're fine."

Love you too. See you Sunday, God willing. We should live and be well.

59.

Michael is seven years older than I am. He remembers hiding under his desk during duck-and-cover drills in elementary school; he remembers being in that same school when he heard the news that President Kennedy was shot. Michael's a full-fledged baby boomer, and I'm on the cusp of Generation X. Along with the difference in our childhood memories, there is also this: he spent his teenage years doing hallucinogenic drugs, and I did not.

"So what was it like?"

We've had many conversations about tripping. Michael's acid trips are, to me, a bit like the experiences he had as a foreign correspondent. He's gone to places I've never been. Seen things I've never seen. And so I ask him—as if for a bulletin from the front of human consciousness.

"It's like seeing at a deeper level," he says. "You see more of what's there. More of what makes everything up."

"Like what?"

"Like . . . I don't know . . . colors. Things moving. Molecules binding together. The pattern behind things." Here he stops, self-conscious.

"And what about after you stop tripping? That pattern—do you feel like what you saw was real?"

"Oh, absolutely. You have no doubt that what you saw was real."

60.

By the second day at Garrison, I felt intimately acquainted with my fellow sojourners, though we hadn't exchanged a single word. We sat, then walked. Sat, then walked. We stood quietly in line for our meals, helped ourselves to tofu stir-fry, brown rice, beet salad. In the absence of human voices, other sounds were magnified: shuffling footsteps, the creak of a floorboard, the clang of silverware. At long tables, we dined next to one another, chewing in silence. The silence itself was a physical presence: a dense, soft blanket that hovered, floating over the dark turrets of the former monastery.

Some people gazed out the high windows at the dull winter sky. Others clasped their hands and bowed their heads in prayer. Still others looked around openly—I was one of these—and gave a small smile and a nod if they caught another person's eye. We might have had very little in common in the outside world, but each of us had chosen these days to retreat, and that choice bound us. We were passengers on the same ship, together in the middle of the ocean.

Sights and sounds grew more intense. As in a sharply rendered pencil drawing, the outlines of my fellow retreatants were stark. A woman with short black hair paced the halls, her face a rictus of apprehension. A bearded man in a baseball cap sat on a bench, holding his head in his hands. A girl—she could have been no more than twenty—dreamily wrote in a notebook decorated with *om* stickers.

After each meal, we wandered slowly back into the meditation hall. People had staked out the prime real estate, leaving a scarf, a pair of glasses, a folded blanket, on a favorite cushion so that they could return to the same spot. In the back row of *zafu*s—with easy access to the door—I left my notebook and pen. The notebook was one I had used, off and on, for a year. It was one of my favorites—writers are nothing if not fetishistic about our notebooks—and I brought it to Garrison with me because it had a few blank pages left.

Sharon and Sylvia took their places in front of the gold Buddha, then waited, looking out over the vast hall as people began to settle back onto their *zafu*s. Stretching, coughing, fidgeting. So hard to be still, even in the silence. *Especially* in the silence. Sylvia adjusted her microphone.

"It's the human dilemma," she began. "Time and the body. It's true that change is always happening."

Change is always happening. So simple. So obvious, really—and at the same time so terrifying. A friend had recently sent me directions to her house, and in describing the way the names of the roads changed for no apparent reason, she had written: *Everything turns into something else.* No wonder I didn't want to think about this. What was the point of thinking about this? Love, joy, happiness—all fleeting. Trying to hold on to them was like grasping at running water.

I reached down for my notebook as Sylvia went on to outline the list, according to the Buddha, of life's vicissitudes:

Pleasure and pain
Gain and loss

Praise and blame
Fame and disrepute

"All lives contain all of these," she said.

All lives. All of these, at one time or another.

I opened my notebook to the last page. As usual, I wanted to write down everything Sylvia said. But something was already scribbled there, in my own handwriting: *Sclerosed introductal papilloma. 4 millimeters. Sports bra.*

The words were in neon. When I wrote them—a year earlier—I had been perched on the edge of the sofa in our library, phone pressed to my ear. My doctor was speaking, her voice calm. *Biopsy. Suspicious. Breast surgeon.* I needed to have breast surgery. There, the notes stopped. A year later, sitting on my meditation cushion in Garrison, I remembered that the doctor had also said not to worry. That it was likely to be nothing. But I didn't write down that part. *Sclerosed. Introductal.* Words I had never seen or used before, written in a shaky hand on the last page of what was, at the time, an empty notebook. A new language. Why had I written on the last page? Could it be that I thought I might have reached the end of my story?

61.

After the surgery—the clean bill of health (*You dodged a bullet, my dear,* the breast surgeon had said)—the rest of the notebook became filled with lists. That fluttering in my stomach, that sick feeling of dread upon awakening each morning during those weeks, mercifully gone. It had been frightening, but in the end, everything was okay. It was a scare, nothing more. Time marched on, while I got back to the stuff of life:

Book Delta flight from Hartford
Read Lee's manuscript
Call Cindy about the boys—play date?
Aunt Shirl—arrange a visit
Jacob—cancel piano

The lists continued, the handwriting neat and orderly, as if perfect penmanship might hold it all together. Packing lists for book tour: *earplugs, computer, power cord, iPhone, charger.* Lists that had to do with my life at home: *pick up sourdough bread, check on FedEx delivery, order party invitations.* Reminders about the school bake sale, camp applications. Notes for speeches, ideas for stories. Random phrases: why had I jotted down *Melbourne?* I had no idea.

"Let's sit for a while." Sylvia's voice pulled me back to the present. The notebook open on my lap, my mind lost in the past. It was time to practice *metta.* The phrases I had learned from Sylvia, the ones I had been using in my meditation practice at home, had been stripped down to their essence over the course of the retreat: *May I be safe, may I be happy, may I be strong, may I live with ease.* I found it easier to sink into the phrases in their pared-down version, with no fancy words, no poetry to get in the way. *Safe.* To be aware of the blessing of physical safety, right here, at this moment—no other. *Happy.* Everything fine, exactly the way it is. *Strong.* Physical fortitude to handle whatever comes. *Live with ease.* Just for now, just for now, just for now.

62.

I was having lunch with an editor who worked at a travel magazine to talk about possible writing assignments. I was a little nervous about the lunch. I didn't have any great ideas for her, and didn't want her to feel like she had wasted her time. I doubted that the magazine—which featured luxury travel—would go for a piece about meditation retreats with scratchy bedding and shared bathrooms. Still, I tried. What about a personal essay on meditating for a week? Or a silent retreat? I worried that it might seem like I was pitching an idea about as interesting as watching water boil.

But then it turned out that the editor herself was a yogi. Quickly—both of us excited to have this common ground—we began talking about the merits of different schools of yoga. She was a devotee of Iyengar; I practiced Anusara. We discussed classes in New York, retreats in Costa Rica, Tuscany, Tulum. As we nibbled on our Turkish food in midtown Manhattan, the world seemed, for a brief moment, to be made up of a small web of people who went into caves and onto mountaintops in search of inner peace.

"India," the editor suddenly exclaimed. "Why don't we send you to India!"

India. My heart sank. How could I tell the travel editor that my interests lay a little closer to home? Say, within a three-hour drive?

She smiled at me from across the table, her eyes twinkling. She knew (and she knew that I knew, and she knew that I knew that she knew) that offering to send a writer to India was a dream assignment. One that most writers would kill for. But not this writer.

India.

For a split second, I wondered: Was this a sign? I hadn't figured out whether or not I believed in signs, though I was working on it. After all, I had followed the trail of breadcrumbs leading me to Steve Cope, to Sylvia Boorstein, to Burt Visotzky. Every experience I'd had was valuable. Some had been transformative. Should I take this moment in the Turkish restaurant as a sign? Get on a plane to New Delhi? Practice yoga and meditation at its birthplace—and get paid for it?

"I can't go to India," I said.

The editor looked surprised.

"Why not?"

"I have a young son," I began, then stopped. It would have been a cop-out to say that it was Jacob who kept me from leaping at the chance to take an all-expenses-paid trip halfway around the world by myself. He was a part of it, sure—a piece of every choice and every decision I made. But motherhood wasn't the whole reason. The truth was that I was tucked into my life, deep into the heart of it. The lessons I needed to learn were all around me. In front of me. Not on the other side of the globe. At least not right now. Did that make my life—my ambitions, my choices—smaller? Or larger?

I imagined myself on the shores of Kerala, in a beautifully embroidered sari, at the feet of my new guru. It should be mentioned that, in this fantasy, I had a pretty good tan. I would gather shining jewels of wisdom from my guru—truths that could be found in no other way—and carry them home in my pocket. But then the fantasy shattered. I saw those jewels falling out of my pocket, one by one. By the time I got back home, back to my life on top of the hill—to my husband, son, dogs, piles upon piles of mail/laundry/manuscripts—I would have left a glittering mess behind me. No longer available. No longer of use. Once again, I was reminded: truths found *out there* don't travel well.

"I think I need to stay close to home," I told the puzzled editor. "My life is here."

63.

I needed to figure out how we could live as Jews in Connecticut, in a part of the state known for its white village churches and horse farms and winding stone walls. We had left the city—along with its hundreds of shuls and kosher delis and more Jewish people on every square block than in most counties across America—and settled in a culture that would have been completely alien to my grandparents, even my parents.

My aunt Shirley recently asked me how Jacob was enjoying school.

"He loves it," I told her. And then tacked on, almost reflexively: "There aren't many Jewish kids there, though."

This was an understatement. Quite possibly, there were no Jewish kids at all.

My aunt looked concerned. "Tell me—is Jacob comfortable with non-Jewish children?"

The question struck me as strange, and underscored the profound difference between Shirley's life and mine. Occasionally, at a school assembly, Michael and I would listen to the surnames of kids called up to the stage for sports or academic awards. Not a single Jewish family. I knew this made both of us a little uneasy. But was Jacob comfortable? You bet he was. He didn't differentiate between Jewish or non-Jewish people. Nor did I really want him to . . . except. Except that we were such a minority.

We were invited to—and participated in—Easter egg hunts, painted, pastel-colored eggs and foil-wrapped candy scattered across lawns. The lone Jews at Christmas dinners, we came bearing gifts to place beneath beautiful trees decorated with twinkling white lights and heirloom ornaments. When Jacob was three, shortly after we had moved, he developed a fascination with churches. They combined several things he loved: bells, clocks, and towers. Often, we stopped on the side of the road if church bells were ringing.

"We're a little bit Christian and a little bit Jewish, right?" he asked hopefully.

"No, honey. We're all Jewish."

"A little bit Christian," he said, as if the subject was closed.

Now, as he slowly—it had happened so fast!—approached the age where if he didn't start Hebrew school, it would become a problem when his bar mitzvah rolled around, we were classic wandering Jews. We had no home, no rabbi, no spiritual institution to call our own.

Half-heartedly, I had done some research over the years. About a thirty-minute drive from our house, off the I-84 corridor, a huge, modern white temple with stained-glass windows overlooked a road lined with antiques stores. It was a Reform congregation, which was very different from the way I had been raised, but did that matter? My religious training hadn't exactly stuck.

"So—what do you think?" I raised the topic of Jacob's religious education with Michael.

He sighed, as if this was a subject he knew had been coming. "I don't know. I really hated Sunday school. I remember being in second grade, and thinking: *Burning bush?* You've got to be fucking kidding me."

"Really? You thought *fucking kidding me* in second grade?"

"You know what I mean."

"Everybody hates Sunday school," I said. I was going on hearsay, of course, since my childhood had been spent in a yeshiva, rendering the whole idea of additional religious training moot.

"So why do it?"

"I want him to know he's Jewish."

"He'll know he's Jewish. His parents are Jewish. His grandparents are Jewish."

"He's not going to get it through osmosis. The kid barely knows what a seder is. And he thinks Hanukkah is about the presents."

"Isn't it?"

"Come on—this is important."

"Okay," Michael said—as I knew he would. It wasn't even really a discussion as much as a ritual dance we had to perform. "Okay."

64.

From the time of our twelve-week sonogram, we knew we were having a boy. Along with the immense, surprising relief I felt flooding me in the doctor's office—there would be no possible repeating of my own history with my mother!—another realization quickly emerged: having a boy meant having a bris.

There never seemed to be any choice in the matter. Certainly I knew that circumcision was a hot-button issue. Was it the healthful thing to do—or a barbaric act? If it should be performed at all, should it be done in a hospital by a trained doctor using anesthetic, or in an unsanitary living room by a religiously ordained mohel? This was not a discussion Michael and I had. We were having a boy. We quickly settled on the name Jacob. And eight days after his birth, a bris would take place, in our living room, complete with catered bagels and lox from Barney Greengrass.

On the morning of Jacob's bris, as our apartment bustled with activity—the food delivery, the flowers, the furniture pushed to the side in anticipation of a crowd—I holed myself up in my bedroom with my baby. Inside his bassinet, his skinny legs stretched out, eyes closed, fingers curling and uncurling, he was perfect. How was it possible that in less than an hour, we would be voluntarily allowing a bearded stranger (I assumed he would be bearded, and he was certainly a stranger) to slice off the skin around the tip of his penis?

Every few minutes, Michael poked his head in to make sure

we were okay. His parents had arrived. A few friends. He was in entertaining mode. I caught a whiff of smoked fish and scallion cream cheese each time he opened the door. I told Michael that we were fine, but if there had been a secret exit, even a fire escape, I might have climbed out my bedroom window and down to the street below. My brand-new mother lion instincts had kicked in, and they didn't involve letting sharp instruments near my eight-day-old infant. I lifted Jacob from his bassinet, then sank in a rocking chair in the corner and nursed him. I couldn't bear the idea that he didn't know what was about to hit him.

As I rocked, I thought about the mohel. We had found him through word of mouth. He was the go-to mohel. Every Jew we knew within a thirty-mile radius had used this guy. The last four digits of his cell phone spelled out B-R-I-S, and when I first called, the outgoing voicemail message announced: "Mazel tov! It's a boy!" He also had a Web site that offered the following options:

If your child has already been born, please click HERE.
If you are a Jewish, Interfaith or Alternative family and you are expecting a baby, please click HERE.
If you are a non-Jewish family looking for the gentlest and most humane approach to circumcising your son, please click HERE.

I tried not to hold it against the mohel that he knew how to market himself. I mean, why not? He was supposed to be the best. But I couldn't help hating him before I had even met him, as if all this was his fault.

The doorbell kept ringing. I stayed in my bedroom with Jacob, figuring they would come get us when they needed us. It seemed to me that the apartment was filled with too many people and their germs. How could it be a good idea to have so many people around a newborn baby? A few friends knocked and tiptoed in—mostly Jewish moms of boys. I could see the sympathy in their eyes; that they knew exactly how I was feeling. They had been here too.

But why? I wanted to wail. *Why do we do this thing? Because our fathers and grandfathers and great-grandfathers did? When is it time to stand down?* I wished my father was alive. If he had been out there in the living room, eating bagels and lox with Michael's parents, at least I would have known why I was doing this—for him. I would have been doing it for him. He would have wrapped his tallit around his big square shoulders and held his firstborn grandson in his arms. He would have worn a royal blue velvet yarmulke, shot through with silver embroidery. He would have said the *bracha*, blessing Jacob as the mohel performed the bris.

Michael opened the bedroom door. Behind him, a tall, bearded man who could only be the mohel. "Don't worry, I haven't lost one yet," the mohel said. Great—a comedian. I carried Jacob, wrapped in a soft blue cotton blanket, into the living room, to a chorus of oohs and aahs, then handed him to my father-in-law. Dozens of people stood holding plates of food. I moved all the way to the back of the room, where I wouldn't be able to see what was happening. Michael stood right next to his father, who sat in a chair and placed Jacob on a pillow.

As the mohel began davening, I closed my eyes and concentrated on my own father, as if the Hebrew words could summon him here. He would have been such a wonderful grandfather: warm and kind and bursting with pride. His absence in the room was palpable. *This is what we do, Dad. Right? We can question it, we can doubt it, we can rail against it—but still, this is what we do.* I wondered if my father ever had questions of his own. Was his acceptance absolute? Was it blind? Did it comfort him—or did it choke him? I would never know. One single piercing cry from Jacob, and it was over. I rushed to the front of the room and bundled him up once again in his soft blue blanket. Back into the bedroom, back to the rocking chair. Through the closed door, I heard the clink of glasses, the scrape of chairs. The sounds of people leaving.

As I held Jacob and kissed away the salty streaks on his cheeks, his wet eyelashes, I felt time move in every direction, expanding outward. We were at the center of something much larger than ourselves. Worlds past and present spun around us. My son, my father, my grandfather, my great-grandfather: links on a chain that connected a dusty Eastern European shtetl to a modern apartment on the Upper West Side.

Was this ancient tradition outmoded? Quite possibly. The mohel had a long, curved pinkie nail (what for?) and used a scalpel that had been his father's. Barbaric? Maybe. Hard to take? Most definitely. But as the guests left and our little family reentered the sleep-deprived weeks of early parenthood, I tried to imagine how it would have been if we *hadn't* had a bris. It wasn't guilt that made me do it. Nor shame, nor even obligation. No. It was simply this: I wanted to stay connected. I didn't want to be the one to break that chain.

65.

The great yogi B. K. S. Iyengar once wrote, "The moment you say 'I have got it,' you have lost everything you had. As soon as something comes, you have to go one step further. Then there is evolution. The moment you say 'I am satisfied with that,' that means stagnation has come. That is the end of your learning; you have closed the windows of your intellect. So let me do what I cannot do, not what I can do."

I was in no danger of self-satisfaction. I had arrived at an understanding of all I could not do, which felt like reaching the edge of the world. Once I realized that the things I had habitually used to prop myself up (the new pair of shoes, the good piece of news, the great review, *whatever*) were as fleeting as a sugar rush, they lost their luster. I had spent years—my whole life!—taping myself together like so many torn bits of paper, bolstering myself up with ephemera. What was I supposed to use to hold myself together, now they were gone? Oh, what's that you say? The idea is not to hold myself together at all?

It felt as if another step, and I would free-fall. Another step, and who knew what would happen? There was no stopping, no pausing. Truly, there was no comfort. How long had I been at this? A year? Two? It was no time at all, in the greater scheme of things, and here I was. I had arrived—in the words of Thomas Merton—at an abyss of irrationality, confusion, pointlessness, and apparent chaos. This, Merton believed, was the only point at which faith was possible. But most days, I felt the chaos without the faith.

I had entered the closest thing to a solitary life that was reasonable for me, given both my nature and my circumstances. I spent my days alone. I didn't answer the phone. I sat at my desk, walked the dogs, got up and stretched, sat back down. I lit a fire in the fireplace, unrolled my mat, practiced yoga. I sat on my *zafu* and meditated for fifteen minutes, twenty. I went back to my desk. Eventually three o'clock rolled around, or four, and it was time for Jacob to come home from school. I didn't know how to transition from one to the other: from hermit to mom. From silence to homework. From inwardness to snack-making and *Honey, how was your day.* I struggled to get inside myself, and then—as if trapped there—I struggled to get back out.

66.

The Hatha Yoga Pradipika, a fifteenth-century text considered to this day to be the classic work on Hatha yoga, was written by an Indian yogi named Svatmarama, about whom little is known. Svatmarama lays out the optimal conditions for the practice of Hatha yoga (*hatha* meaning simply the physical practice of yoga) in the following way:

"The Hatha yogi should live in a secluded hut free of stones, fire, and dampness to a distance of four cubits in a country which is properly governed, virtuous, prosperous and peaceful. These are the marks of a yoga hut as described by masters practicing Hatha:

a small door, no windows, no rat holes; not too high, too low, or too long; well-plastered with cow dung, clean and bug free. The grounds are enclosed by a wall, and beautified by an arbor, a raised platform, and a well. Living in this hut, free of all anxieties, one should earnestly practice yoga as taught by one's guru."

67.

The tumors in my mother's brain looked like dust, sprinkled there on the black-and-white lunar landscape of the X-ray. The oncologist pointed to them with the tip of his pencil. "There," he said. "Do you see that? And there." He kept moving his pencil. Finally I began to see that the grayish blur he was showing us was actually dozens—maybe hundreds—of minuscule tumors.

"So how do we get rid of them?" asked my mother.

I sat next to her, close enough to touch. Her winter coat was folded in her lap, and her cane rested against the side of the oncologist's desk. For the first time, my mother looked brittle, as if her bones might break from a fall.

"We don't," the doctor answered. "We can treat them, but . . ." He trailed off, shrugging his shoulders as if to say that these specks were too much for him.

"Mostly, Mrs. Shapiro, what we can do at this point is make you comfortable."

"Comfortable," my mother repeated.

I focused on the doctor's coffee mug. *I'd Rather Be Driving a Mercedes,* it read. Despite his taste in mugs, I liked this guy. He was the fourth oncologist my mother had been through, and I hoped she wouldn't get rid of him as well. He was more honest, more direct, than the others had been.

"Mom, do you understand what the doctor is saying?" I asked. No one had actually come out and used the D word. Death was delivered one euphemistic blow at a time: *comfortable, palliative, nothing more we can do.*

"I think it's time to talk about hospice care," the doctor said.

My mother didn't flinch. "That's it, then."

I reached over and held my mother's hand. Her skin was papery, thin. An old woman's hand. According to what I could sort out from the Internet, she had a couple of good months left. The terrible mess of our past no longer mattered. Those sessions in the therapist's office were a distant memory. There was no hope for our relationship, at this late date. "No hope at all," the therapist had said. I had no illusions that now, in some final and dramatic flash of revelation, we would understand one another. We were done. It was a fact of my life—intractable and sad—that our relationship had been a failure. Still, with her prognosis came one last chance to be her daughter.

But what did that mean, to be my mother's daughter? I wasn't sure what she wanted or needed of me. Of course, there were the practical matters. The home health aides, hospice nurses, accountants, lawyers. The paperwork, as if death could be arranged in carefully labeled file folders. The power of attorney, the safe deposit box, the bank statements. The sudden physical intimacy: the nakedness, the commode, the bedpan.

Years earlier—as a twenty-three-year-old—I had rented my mother an apartment and furnished it so that she would have a place to start her new life as a widow in New York. At the time, I wondered what would happen to her. She was still quite young. She had money. She was smart, and beautiful. Would she find herself? Possibly have a second act? Would she stop being so angry at the world? I had hoped she would change. But then the years tumbled by in a blur of sadness and blame. Now—a long time and several apartments later—all she wanted to talk about was the dispersal of stuff. She had spent a lifetime collecting fine things, and wanted to be sure I'd take good care of them after she was gone.

The Nakashima table is worth a lot of money.

There's vintage Pucci in the closet.

That painting should be reappraised.

She walked unsteadily from one corner of her apartment to the other, pointing out objects of value, and I followed her, pen in hand. Of course, this was the easy part, if there was an easy part. This, I could do. I kept lists upon lists. *Nakashima—look up mid-century modern dealers. Pucci—consignment? Call insurance agent.* These were my acts of devotion. *Armani jacket in closet—tags still attached. Return to Bergdorf?*

Well-meaning acquaintances would occasionally suggest that my mother and I had an opportunity for closure. That this could be a healing time. They didn't know my mother or our history. It was something you say in these situations. Along with *God doesn't give us more than we can handle* and *Everything happens for a reason* came the idea that surely, between a dying mother and her only child, there would be important moments to be shared. Private sorrows, joys, admissions, apologies.

Instead, I took notes. *Eames chair*, I carefully wrote. *Original upholstery. Turkish rug from the 1930s. Hand-blown glass from Jerusa-*

lem. I can still hear my mother telling me, with the tremendous urgency of a confession: "Don't forget, Dani—the pearls are good."

68.

The message popped up on my screen one freezing cold morning. I was at my desk, nursing my second cup of coffee. The house, quiet. The dogs asleep at my feet. The e-mail was from someone I barely knew.

TO: DANI SHAPIRO

SUBJECT: FWD: PRAYER

I am supposed to pick twelve women (who have touched my life) and whom I think would want to participate. I hope I chose the right twelve. Please send this back to me (you'll see why). In case anyone is not aware, St. Theresa is known as the Saint of the Little Ways. Meaning she believed in doing the little things in life well and with great love. She is also the patron Saint of flower growers and florists. She is represented by roses. REMEMBER to make a wish before you read the prayer. That's all you have to do. There is nothing attached. Just send this to twelve people and let me know what happens on the fourth day. Sorry you have to forward the message, but try not to break this, please. Prayer is one of the best free gifts we receive. Did you make your wish yet? If you don't make a wish, it won't come true. This is your last chance to make a wish!

I hated getting e-mails like this, because they made me feel guilty—like I should somehow participate. For a moment, I tried to think of twelve friends who wouldn't mind receiving it. I couldn't even come up with one. *Last chance to make a wish.* That wasn't a very nice thing to impose on a friend, was it? Wishes, prayer, confusion, guilt—all wrapped up in one tidy little paragraph. *If you don't make a wish, it won't come true.* I deleted the e-mail. I sat there and stared at my screen. Then I pulled it out of my trash. But I didn't send it on.

69.

Does a seeker ever stop seeking? Or is the very definition of a seeker one who keeps searching, driven by an insatiable hunger for knowledge, awareness, wisdom, peace? The very idea of craving peace struck me as vaguely oxymoronic. Craving, after all, was the antithesis of all things peaceful. It meant living with a constant itch. A dissatisfaction with *what is.* But could there be such a thing as spiritual satisfaction?

Some days, during my yoga practice, when I played the CD mix Michael had made for me, invariably I found myself in *vashistasana,* or side plank pose, listening to the lyrics from the Eagles song *Desperado*: "It seems to me some fine things have been laid upon your table, but you only want the ones that you can't get." As I lifted up into side plank, balancing on one hand, focusing on the treetops in the distance, I promised myself I wouldn't be like that. I would recognize the fine things on my table. I wouldn't want the ones I couldn't get. Wanting more meant *upadana*, the Pali word for clinging, which translates literally into "fuel." Clinging, craving, desiring, all add fuel to the fire of suffering.

I wondered if there was an end to the journey—other than the obvious Big End. Certainly, I knew people who were all set. My aunt Shirley and her entire brood, for instance. They didn't question whether Judaism was the answer for them. They were Jewish! It was the answer! Their lives were lived in shuls and around Shabbos tables, and if they had questions and doubts, those were framed within the context of their Judaism. I thought of occasional people I had encountered along the way: Jews, yogis, Buddhists, Christians, who seemed to be absolutely sure they were in the right place.

At lunch with Steve Cope, in the Kripalu cafeteria, over steamed kale and hot water with lemon, I brought up these questions once again. What did it mean, to have arrived at a place that felt real and right and true? Was there an end to seeking? Or was it simply a matter of saying, *Okay, this is good enough. I'm stopping here?*

Steve leaned across the table, as if telling me a secret. "You know, there's an ancient Christian mystical teaching about being one with the flame," he said. "The flame is always there—call it whatever you want . . . God, the Holy Spirit—but the idea is that we try to bring ourselves into alignment with it."

I thought about this for a moment. All around us in the enormous cafeteria, Kripalu guests were eating healthy lunches, before returning to their programs: "Coyote Healing: The Power of Native American Spirituality." "The Self behind the Symptom: How Shadow Voices Heal Us." Everyone was hoping to feel better. Everyone was seeking something.

"But what would happen if you became one with the flame all the time?" I asked Steve. "Wouldn't it be too intense? Wouldn't you . . . I don't know . . . burn yourself up?"

Steve took a sip of tea, then smiled.

"Oh, I don't think we need to worry about that," he said. "You can put that at the bottom of your list."

70.

We joined the huge modern white synagogue near the highway. It seemed like the thing to do. The synagogue had a Hebrew school—the only one I was aware of within a thirty-minute drive. So I wrote a painfully large check, and Jacob began his twice-a-week religious education, which seemed to mostly entail bringing home arts and crafts projects like laminated place mats decorated with the Hebrew alphabet, and quarter-annual badge ceremonies held on Sunday mornings, in which the kids sang Israeli folk songs and parents were handed sheets with the transliteration, so we could sing along.

Months went by, and we hadn't attended a service. There was always a reason: a late piano lesson, a dinner plan. The truth was, it wasn't a priority. But increasingly I felt like we had to at least *try*. Each week, I received e-mails inviting us to one event or another: *Learn how to cook, Jewish-style! Moms' Night Out! Come shmooze and check out our Hanukkah boutique!* What was the point of sending Jacob to Hebrew school if we weren't going to be part of the community? We had to do this. Given that we had chosen to live here in Cheever country, it was up to us to reach out.

Michael, Jacob, and I piled into the car and drove to the synagogue early one Friday evening. As we walked from the parking lot into the glass-walled entrance of the main building, I felt like we were in the wrong place. I tried to shake my mood, but this place didn't feel like shul to me. There were no men in black coats and yarmulkes. No women and children dressed in their nice clothes. That brisk, efficient bustle that I associated with the onset of Shabbos was lost amid the SUVs and minivans in the suburban parking lot. As we entered the main sanctuary, I scanned the room. Not a soul looked familiar.

We slid into the back row and waited for services to begin. Jacob was already squirming. Michael was squirming too.

"Come on, guys. Let's try to have a good attitude," I said, as much to myself as to them. I pulled out the siddur to take a look at it. Almost the entire prayer book was in English.

The rabbi climbed three stairs to the bimah, and stood at the pulpit. He was a small man, bald under his yarmulke.

"Shabbat Shalom!" he greeted the congregation.

"Shabbat Shalom!" the group called back.

The service began. I had been looking forward to this part. The singing, the music, always brought my father back to me. At pretty much any Jewish service, I could close my eyes and feel him in the room. His voice, his warmth, the scent of his tallit. My childhood was always available to me in the language of the siddur.

"We will read responsively," said the rabbi. He cleared his throat.

"Come my Beloved to greet the bride," he read.

"The Sabbath presence, let us welcome," responded the congregation.

Oh, *no.* Was the whole service going to be in English? In my mind, the familiar strains of "Lecha Dodi" played like background music. *Lecha Dodi, likrat kalah, penei Shabbat nekabela . . .*

I could hardly sit still. The entire service went on this way, punctuated by occasional singing by a female cantor, which seemed more like an operatic performance than a ritual of prayer. At a few points, the congregation was asked to sing a little something— usually comprised of *lai, lai, lai.* People swayed and put their arms around each other. The next thing I knew—what the hell was happening?—congregants had stood and formed a large circle, and were doing some sort of Israeli folk dance. A woman wearing a tallit and a helmet-sized embroidered yarmulke was leading the dancing.

"Help," Michael whispered in my ear.

Jacob was kicking the back of the pew in front of us. I had made him wear nice shoes to go to synagogue. All the other kids were in sneakers—a fact which had not gone unnoticed by him. My guys were not happy with me, not at all.

"Mommy, what time is it?" Jacob asked. It was his way of asking how much more he'd have to endure.

"It'll be a while, sweetie."

The conga line swirled around us. The yarmulke lady threw back her head as she danced. I wondered how the yarmulke stayed put. Here, in a suburban shul off the interstate highway, was a whole form of Judaism to which I hadn't been exposed. It was . . . *ecstatic.* It reminded me of people I had seen on TV, speaking in tongues or falling to their knees in fits of religious fervor. And yet there was something so ersatz about it. Ersatz ecstasy. I wanted to bolt.

But we couldn't leave. I mean, what kind of message would that send to Jacob—that his parents thought it was okay to sneak out of shul? The rabbi returned to the dais and faced the congregation. It was sermon time.

"On this Shabbat, as we read the Torah portion, I find myself thinking about Alex Rodriguez," he began.

Michael squeezed my hand hard. *A-Rod?* I wasn't sure which was worse: that the rabbi was using a baseball player to illustrate the Torah portion, or that he was a Yankees fan.

"When A-Rod plays, what we see is incredible determination—"

"Okay," I whispered to Michael. I nudged Jacob to get up. "Let's get out of here."

We slid from the last row. The three of us tiptoed out like teenagers.

71.

The calls came a couple of times a year. A halting voice on the answering machine: *Hi, Ms. Shapiro. You don't know me, but I'm a friend of _____'s. We're in the hospital right now with our baby who has been diagnosed with infantile spasms.* The brokenness of the voice was unmistakable. This was a mother or a father willing to go down any road, to make any call, to try *anything* if it might give their child a chance of survival.

Sometimes I was contacted by e-mail—the subject line something like *I.S.—Please Help!!!* Michael and I had created a Web page where we told the story of Jacob's recovery. The page featured a photograph of Jacob at age three, his eyes huge, sparkling—full of life. I hoped that parents who were desperately searching for information about infantile spasms in the middle of the night might stumble on it, and see that a positive outcome wasn't completely impossible. Back when I had been the one searching, click after merciless click, there were no such stories.

I kept in mind my friend's friend—the one whose son had ended up at Dartmouth. The fact of her unwillingness to speak to me about her experience was incomprehensible to me. Oh, I understood her desire for privacy, and her fear of the pain she might experience on revisiting her son's long-ago illness. But how could she not have known that talking about it would *help*, actually—not only me, but herself?

Each time I ended a phone call or an e-mail correspondence with an IS parent, I felt emotionally drained, exhausted, and sad. Most of their babies wouldn't make it. The seizures would leave them brain-damaged, blind, physically impaired. They were being treated by doctors who weren't willing to take the risk of using the experimental medication that had saved Jacob. It wasn't FDA-approved, after all. Worse still, some babies were in clinical trials for that very same medication—on subclinical doses. Their parents were lost, baffled. Should they look for a new doctor? Risk alienating the one they already had? Their stories stirred up the old terror, the latent fear—and yet, what I felt beneath all that was the simple beauty of human connection. The consolation, in the words of the poet Jane Kenyon, of one soul extending to another soul and saying, *I've been there too.* It wasn't everything, but it was something—wasn't it? The reaching out—needing to believe that a hand would be there?

72.

Seventy-two. According to the Kabbalah, God has seventy-two names. A friend had signed me up for a weekly Kabbalah tune-up e-mail from a rabbi in Beverly Hills. Each week, I opened a new e-mail to find a new name, there in bold Hebrew letters. "Scan from right to left" was the helpful suggestion. That week's name was accompanied by a New Age meditation: *I find the strength to restrain selfish longing. Through this Name I ask for what my soul needs, not what my ego wants.* The whole thing made me feel like I was playing with voodoo, and eventually I stopped opening the e-mails.

One longs for a device that is not a trick, Virginia Woolf wrote in her diary. Still, lists seemed important. I liked making lists. Numbers were meaningful. Eighteen, for *chai.* Twenty-three, for the age I was when I lost my father. One in seven million, for the odds of Jacob having fallen ill.

The story of the seventy-two names originates in Exodus 14, verses 19–21. Israelites stood at the shore of the Red Sea. The Egyptians were closing in on them. They were trapped—they had nowhere to go. They cried out to God, asking for his help. And this was God's answer: *Why are you calling out to me?* I had always thought God's response to the Israelites to be typical of him. *Who are you talking to? What makes you think I'm listening? I've got better things to do.* That was certainly the God I had grown up with: if he was paying attention at all, it was a punishing kind of attention. But as I explored the story of the seventy-two names, I began to understand it differently.

Why are you calling out to me? God was imploring the Israelites to look elsewhere, because the answer was right in front of them. At the moment they were helplessly calling out to God, Moses revealed the seventy-two names. These names pierced the collective soul of the Israelites, who began marching into the waters of the Red Sea. On they went into the churning depths, and when they had reached the point of near-drowning, when there was no turning back—*Faith is the substance of things hoped for, the evidence of things not seen*—then, and only then, did the waters part.

73.

Before Jacob turned six months old, people started to ask when we were going to have another one. I was thirty-seven. We didn't have much time. *Better get going! What are you waiting for?* Something about new motherhood seemed to allow for these questions. I had almost gotten used to the way that pregnancy and nursing had turned my body into a subject that was apparently open for discussion. "Any day now!" my doorman would say each morning I lumbered past him to collect the mail. Mothers at the playground—bleary-eyed, sleep-deprived—lived in a universe where no subject was too personal. *How long are you planning to breast-feed? How was the birth?* But the questions about another baby irritated me. I felt quick flashes of irrational fury every time someone asked. *None of your business,* I wanted to say. Why did everyone assume we'd have another baby? Maybe we had no intention of having another baby! Maybe we were planning to have just one.

I kept a mental list of only children I had known. In particular, I kept a mental list of happy, smart, contented, successful only children I had known. It wasn't a long list, but it comforted me. I had been an only child myself. (Well, there was my half-sister, but she was so much older than me, and we had never lived under the same roof.) When I was a kid, I had longed for a brother or sister. Whenever I thought about having—or not having—another baby, my own childhood self rose up and confronted me.

You have to have another one.

No, I don't.

You'll be repeating history.

It wasn't all bad.

Didn't you always want a gaggle of kids?

Oh, that was a childhood fantasy.

But the truth is that I was terrified. I was a big believer in not pushing my luck. I viewed Jacob—perfect, beautiful, healthy Jacob—as the greatest possible piece of good fortune. I wanted a baby and had one. The pregnancy had been unremarkable. From the time of his birth, I had marveled at him. Ten fingers and ten toes! Legs and arms and a little round head! Knees and ankles and elbows! Despite the fact that women had been giving birth for quite a few centuries, deep within myself I hadn't believed that it would be possible for me. Still, I didn't completely rule out the idea of another child. I told myself that I had time. Thirty-seven, thirty-eight, thirty-nine . . . women were having babies into their forties, weren't they? The world seemed increasingly populated by fertility twins.

Then Jacob got sick. His illness took the question of another baby off the table. All of my energy was devoted to making him better. The year of medication passed. Then the year of catching up: the speech therapy, the occupational therapy, the endless worry. We left the city. We moved to the country. My mother was dying. And then there was the ultimate frightening question: Were infantile spasms hereditary? It didn't seem so—but so little was understood about the condition. No one could say, for sure.

Eventually, much to my relief, people stopped asking. But I didn't stop thinking about it. Another baby? Did I dare? It had become the central question, a steady hum beneath all other thoughts. One beautiful fall day, I glanced out my office window and saw Jacob in the front meadow, kicking a soccer ball by himself, and something went through me—a pang so sharp my breath caught in my throat. He *had* to have a brother or sister. What I felt—my own fears and worries—simply didn't matter.

Michael and I started talking about it. "I've never regretted what I have done," he said at one point. "Only what I haven't." I knew he was right. It seemed there was an empty seat at our table. Did I want to look back, some day, and know that it was fear that had stopped me? Risk was everywhere. Getting out of bed in the morning was a risk. Driving the car down the driveway was a risk. Turning on the stove to cook dinner was a risk. I wanted a crystal ball, a guarantee—but I knew there were no guarantees. Not of anything, not at any time. *Pleasure and pain, gain and loss, praise and blame, fame and disrepute*, as the Buddhists say. *All lives contain all of these.*

Moving through fear is its own leap of faith. And so, at forty, I closed my eyes and leapt.

74.

The Pali word *dukkha*—often translated as "suffering"—is central to Buddhist teachings. When Siddhartha Gautama (otherwise known as Buddha) emerged, enlightened, from his spot beneath the Bodhi tree, he offered the first of the Four Noble Truths, which is that life is *dukkha*: "Birth is *dukkha*, aging is *dukkha*, death is *dukkha*; sorrow, lamentation, pain, grief and despair are *dukkha*; association with the unbeloved is *dukkha*; separation from the loved is *dukkha*; not getting what is wanted is *dukkha*. In short, the five clinging-aggregates are *dukkha*."

Modern translators warn against the idea that there is one correct translation for *dukkha*. The word itself, it seems, is bottomless. According to a contemporary definition by the Buddhist scholar Francis Story, *dukkha* is: "Disturbance, irritation, dejection, worry, despair, fear, dread, anguish, anxiety; vulnerability, injury, inability, inferiority; sickness, aging, decay of the body and faculties, senility; pain/pleasure; excitement/boredom; deprivation/excess; desire/frustration, suppression; longing/aimlessness; hope/hopelessness; effort, activity, striving/repression; loss, want, insufficiency/satiety; love/lovelessness, friendlessness; dislike, aversion/attraction; parenthood/childlessness; submission/rebellion; decision/indecisiveness, vacillation, uncertainty."

75.

My mother did not want to be buried in the Shapiro family plot. She hadn't been too fond of my father's family when they were alive, and wasn't keen on spending eternity with them. "I'm sorry for you," she told me, sounding anything but. "You'll have to visit your parents in two different cemeteries."

It started this way—the planning of her own death—with an outpouring of fury. She threatened to disown me and leave her estate to Dorot, a Jewish eldercare organization with headquarters around the corner from her apartment. She changed her will multiple times. She made arrangements to be buried next to her parents in southern New Jersey, rather than next to "those people." Still, as death approached, my mother grew slowly sweeter. As the terrible noise that must have been inside her head subsided, suddenly there was space to see the world, not as the unwelcoming place she had always imagined it, but as it really was.

One afternoon, she came by car service to visit us at our house in Connecticut. We all knew it would be her last visit. She was beginning to fail. First her legs went, then her balance, then memory, one story at a time. She was in a wheelchair, bald from radiation, wearing a jaunty hat. It was an early spring day, warm enough to sit outside. We wheeled her around the back of the house, and she and I sat there, blankets around our shoulders, and watched Michael and Jacob throw around a football. My mother observed them quietly. What was she seeing? A beautiful child running, laughing. A doting husband and father, tackling him. The snow-drops—delicate white buds—beneath the tree out back, beginning to bloom. I kept looking at my mother out of the corner of my eye. She was shaking her head slightly, smiling. Gone was the judgment (*Shouldn't Jacob be wearing a warmer jacket? The house sure could use a paint job, couldn't it?*). Gone was the reflexive need to see the worst in things. Before the tumors took her life, they gave her a few moments of grace.

"Michael's a good father," she said, turning to me in surprise. Her face, caught in a bright angle of sunlight, was soft and vulnerable. It was the first kind thing she had ever said about my husband. A few weeks later, she slipped permanently into unconsciousness.

76.

I met Sylvia Boorstein for an early dinner one cold, wet night in New York. I had been looking forward to it for weeks. We sat at a window table in a restaurant in the Time Warner Center, overlooking Columbus Circle, the headlights of cars flitting in all directions like so many fireflies. The world outside, which moments earlier had felt oppressive to me—freezing, crowded, too loud—now looked inviting from our cozy perch.

Sylvia had become, in a short span of time, very dear to me. As was the case the first time I heard her speak at Kripalu, her words seemed to enter me without dilution, deflection—without my turning them around and examining them to decide what was true. *Everything* was true. And so as we sat together over our Niçoise salad and vegetable risotto, I tried to stay in the moment. Not to be thinking: *How much time do we have left? When will I see her again? She lives in northern California, so far away. She's getting older. What if something happens to her?* I tried not to lean so far into the future that I squandered the present.

We caught each other up on our lives: Sylvia's teaching, my work, our travels. We talked about a particularly wonderful Alice Munro story we had both recently read in the *New Yorker*. The final sentence of the story—*I grew up, and old*—had stayed with me. Is that what happens? We grow up, then old? The story had touched on a constant, gnawing sadness that was always with me. This sadness wasn't a huge part of me—I wasn't remotely depressed—but still, it was like a stone I carried in my pocket. I always knew it was there.

"I think of it as the edge of melancholy," Sylvia said, "and it's where I live—but at the same time I am easily cheered." Where else was a sensible person to live, but on the edge of sorrow? I pictured myself and Sylvia, on some sort of window ledge, our legs gaily dangling beneath us. Not falling over, but all the while aware that a world of pain simmered below. Sylvia had written beautifully about this: "In the best of circumstances, a loving family, good health, adequate financial resources, and untroubled times are the palace walls that protect our childhoods and early consciousness and allow us to move into our adult lives with confidence. And then, sooner or later, we see what the Buddha saw. We see the truth of change. We begin to understand how fragile life is and how, most surely, we will lose everything that is dear to us. At some point, in some way, we ask ourselves this question: 'What is to be done? Is there some way I can do this life with my eyes open and my heart open and still love it? Is there a way not to suffer?'"

Our waitress came by with refills for our coffee. Plates were cleared, dessert offered. I fought the urge to look at my watch. I felt the way Jacob sometimes feels when he's having a really good time. He always worries about the endings of things, even as they are beginning. He gets it from me. But now, I resisted the future's tug. I was right there, right then, with a remarkable woman whom I was lucky to know.

"I'm always aware of time passing—of loss, coming around the corner," I said to Sylvia as we sipped our coffee. "Whether it's being middle-aged, or watching Jacob grow up, or seeing my in-laws getting old, or even this dinner—" I stopped. This was it. What the Buddha saw: the fragility of life, the truth of change. Whether something small and simple, like dinner with a special friend, or something unbearable to contemplate, like the loss of loved ones, change was inevitable. Change was happening right at this very minute.

Sylvia was nodding, smiling her beatific smile. Beaming with empathy. "I remember, after my father was diagnosed with cancer, I watched him one day struggling with his cane, and suddenly I saw the father of my childhood," she said. "We used to go to Coney Island when I was a little girl, and he was a very athletic guy—he used to walk on his hands into the ocean. And I saw that young man walking on his hands, and the old man who was walking with a cane . . ." She trailed off. We both looked at each other. We were talking about painful things, and yet I think both of us felt unaccountably happy. *Easily cheered.* This sharing, this acknowledgment of what it is to be human—this was the faint light of hope from the edge of melancholy.

We settled the check, then hugged good night. The time we had together—as Jacob would put it—had flown by. I took a deep breath. The *metta* phrases I learned from Sylvia ran through my mind, in what had become habit. *May I be safe; may I be happy; may I be strong; may I live with ease.* I rode the escalator down, past brightly lit shops and restaurants. Outside, on Columbus Circle, Sylvia would be getting into a taxi. *May you be safe; may you be happy; may you be strong; may you live with ease.* I directed the phrases at my friend as she headed back uptown. I hoped—it was all I could do—that we would meet many times again.

77.

So what *is* to be done? It was the question at the core of all the questions I had been asking. Life is suffering. There is no way around it. The human condition—the knowledge of this—drives many of us to drink, to drugs, to denial, to running as fast as we can away from the truth of life's fragility. We think we can shore ourselves up. If only we work hard enough, make lots of money, are good and kind enough, pray hard enough, we will somehow be exempt. Then we discover that no one is exempt. What is to be done?

The key word was *doing.* Not thinking, or wishing, or contemplating. Not staring into space. Not succumbing to dismay. Recently I went to see a friend, a psychopharmacologist, because I had begun to wonder if thinking about all this stuff all the time was making me unwell. "You're not having a chemical crisis, Dani," he told me. "You're having an existential crisis."

It wasn't getting easier because it isn't supposed to get easier. Midlife was a bitch, and my educated guess was that the climb only got steeper from here. Carl Jung put it perfectly: "Thoroughly unprepared we take the step into the afternoon of life," he wrote. "Worse still, we take this step with the false assumption that our truths and ideals will serve us as hitherto. But we cannot live the afternoon of life according to the program of life's morning; for what was great in the morning will be little at evening, and what in the morning was true will by evening have become a lie."

Doing was what was necessary. Action has magic, grace, and power in it, as Goethe once wrote. Whenever I took an action—yoga or meditation practice, trying a new shul, reading a bit from the Buddhist wisdom book to Jacob in the morning, expressing gratitude at the dinner table—I felt . . . better. I was writing a new program for the afternoon of life. The scales tipped away from suffering and toward openheartedness and love.

78.

I climbed the stairs to the glass front doors of the Jewish Theological Seminary in upper Manhattan, carrying a shopping bag. Inside the bag were several velvet pouches, embroidered with silver and gold thread.

"I have an appointment to see Rabbi Visotzky," I told the guard. I was surprised—though I shouldn't have been—by the high level of security. My bag and I passed through a metal detector and into the lobby, where I waited for Burt.

A few weeks earlier, he and I had been having coffee when he asked me if I still had my father's tallit and tefillin. I was certain that they were somewhere in my house; probably boxed up in the basement. I didn't stop to wonder why Burt was asking. But before we got up to leave the cafe, he circled back around to the subject.

"I say this in full awareness of the responsibility it entails," he said. His intense dark eyes were even more intense than usual. "If you would like me to teach you to put on your father's tefillin, I would be honored."

I felt a kind of slamming inside; doors blew open and closed at once. Put on my father's tefillin? Heat rose to my face. It was forbidden territory—so off-limits as to seem almost sexual. But on the other hand, here was one of the greatest minds in modern Judaism offering me a profound learning experience. There was no way I was going to say no, though the thought of it undid me. What would my father think? In the 1970s, when women were first allowed to read from the Torah in Conservative synagogues, my father would quietly walk out of the temple when a woman approached the ark. He did this not in protest, but because it wasn't in line with his beliefs. And though he never said it, I think it offended him. Women were not meant to perform aliyahs, read from the Torah, become rabbis or cantors. Daughters were most certainly not supposed to schlep their father's tefillin to the Jewish Theological Seminary in a shopping bag on the invitation of a rabbi famous for starting the seminary's first egalitarian service.

Burt met me in the lobby, then led me upstairs through a labyrinth of halls. He had been at the seminary for his whole adult life. He walked briskly around corners, opened doors to hidden passageways leading to his book-lined office. All the while, I followed him, feeling frightened but also exhilarated. Back home, at the kitchen table, shaking the dust out of my father's tallit and carefully wiping the straps of his tefillin with leather cleaner, I had felt the whole of my history brush up against me.

We made no small talk. The mood between us was serious as I unzipped the velvet pouches and laid my father's tefillin out on Burt's desk. The straps were brittle and retained their shape from having been wound around the wooden boxes that protected the phylacteries for the past twenty years. The boxes weren't in the best condition. The Hebrew letters stenciled onto them had faded, though they could still be made out. But inside, the phylacteries themselves were perfectly preserved.

"This is the head tefillin." Burt held up one of the two boxes. "The Hebrew says *shel rosh*—for the head." He examined the other box. "And this one is *shel yad*—for the arm." He looked more closely at the two boxes and the way the straps had been wound. "Was your father a lefty?"

I was surprised to realize that I didn't remember. This was an awful feeling—this not remembering. How could I not know if my father had been left-handed? It suddenly seemed a critical fact about him that I had been robbed of by his death. One more thing I didn't know.

"I could call my aunt Shirley and ask," I said. But then I thought better of it. I didn't want to explain to Shirley that I was in a rabbi's office learning to lay tefillin.

"No need," Burt said. "Do you have the tallit?"

I pulled out my father's tallit from its pouch. During my wedding to Michael, we had used it as our chuppah. If my father would never meet my husband, at least we could be married beneath the tallit he had worn all his life. The embroidery around its border had yellowed, and the fringes I remembered playing with as a little girl were tangled and frayed.

"Do you want to wear a yarmulke?" Burt asked.

Somehow, a yarmulke seemed like overkill. I shook out the tallit's folds, then pulled it over my head like a hood, crossing it over my face. I closed my eyes and breathed in any little bit of my father that might exist inside his tallit and said my own version of a prayer: *Hope this is okay, Dad.* Then I let it settle around my shoulders. My father had been a large man, and I was enveloped by his tallit. It nearly reached the floor.

"Baruch atah adonai," I recited with Burt. My father's voice said the blessing along with us. He faced the windows in our New Jersey den, his Wall Street shoes shiny and ready to go. "Eloheinu melech ha'olam asher kidshanu b'mitzvotav v'tzivanu l'hitateif ba tzitzit."

"Now the tefillin. We start with your left arm." I awkwardly placed the phylactery over my bicep as Burt led me through the blessing over laying tefillin. I was wearing a sleeveless blouse, and suddenly wished my arms were covered. The worn leather strap against my bare skin looked alien and strange. I wound it from my bicep to my wrist, then held the remaining length of the strap loosely in my hand.

Burt helped me to place *ha-rosh*, the head tefillin, correctly so that the phylactery was at the top of my hairline, and the knot at the bottom of the strap's loop nestled into the hollow at the base of my skull. His office was dead quiet; the thick walls of the seminary blocked out all sounds of traffic from Broadway down below. I felt disembodied. Floating outside myself—my feelings too intense and conflicted. Why was I doing this? Was it wrong? Burt tightened the loop around my head slightly so that it fit. Then he showed me how to wrap the remaining length of the strap in my hand: around the middle finger, twice on the lower joint and once on the middle joint. The rest was then wound around my palm, the lines of the straps crisscrossing, emulating Hebrew letters. The result of this intricate process spelled out one of God's names: *Shadai.*

"The strap wound around your finger symbolizes an act of betrothal to God," said Burt. With him, I recited the final blessing: "I will betroth you unto Me forever; I will betroth you unto Me in righteousness and in justice and in kindness and in compassion; I will betroth you unto Me in faithfulness."

But it didn't feel like God to whom I was betrothing myself. If anything, I felt like my father's bride. He had bound himself to God; I had bound myself to him. There, in a rabbi's study above Broadway, I felt the power and intensity of my connection to my father, as I stood wrapped in his tallit and tefillin.

"How does it feel?" asked Burt.

"Very strange," I answered. "It feels like a costume."

"It *is* a costume. As far back as Juvenal the Satirist, there is record of pagan women wearing Jewish amulets. *Phylacteries* come from the same root as *prophylactic,*" said Burt. "Something that guards you. They also say that if you wrap yourself in tefillin and have a mezuzah on your door, you're protected from harm." He paused. "Would that it were so."

Would that it were so. My father had performed this ritual every weekday morning of his life from the time of his bar mitzvah. It hadn't kept him from harm. But the tefillin were accoutrements of prayer, and the donning of them, a form of moving meditation. Maybe this simple, repetitive act gave my father courage, each morning, to face the day. Maybe it reminded him of who he was and what was important to him. And maybe, through his example, he taught me a lesson about the importance of a daily connection to that deeper place.

79.

The Sanskrit word for devotion is *bhakta*. It comes from the verbal root *bhaj*, which is defined as: (1) distributed, allotted, assigned; (2) divided; (3) served, worshipped; (4) engaged; (5) attached or devoted to, loyal, faithful; (6) dressed, cooked (as in food); (7) forming a part of, belonging to; (8) loved, liked.

80.

It took several months to clean out my mother's apartment. She had lived in a converted three-bedroom in a new building on West Eighty-sixth Street. The apartment had a reasonable number of closets, especially by Manhattan standards, but still, my mother had built additional walls of closets in the master bedroom, the kitchen, and her office.

I hardly knew where to begin. The kitchen seemed safest, least personal. Aside from the three sets of china, the good silver, the Danish stainless, the dozens of sets of salt and pepper shakers, my mother had kept every plastic doily and Chinese food container that had ever been delivered to her. She threw away nothing—made no distinction between valuable items and what might have arguably been considered trash. Many of the kitchen cupboards were piled high with cashmere sweaters of every color and weight. Some, folded with tissue paper and laid flat in vinyl bags, were from the 1940s, when she had been a sorority girl. Others had never been worn; some still had Saks Fifth Avenue price tags attached. In the top cupboards, which required a step-ladder to reach, there was a collection of hatboxes from midtown milliners who had long since gone out of business: a leopard pill-box, straw boaters, an enormous sable thing.

What to do? What to do with any of it? All that long, hot summer, I kept lists and made piles. *Keep, store, toss.* It was my griev-ing process, I suppose. I wasn't so much mourning the loss of my mother as coming face-to-face with the absolute end of our story. The sharp sliver of hope I had always kept with me, despite what I knew, despite what anyone said—that sliver had shattered. I would be finding the embedded shards—*samskaras*—for the rest of my life. Meanwhile, the piles grew. *Keep, store, toss.* I called vin-tage dealers, consignment stores. I carted garbage bags full of de-signer clothes to a second-floor shop across town where Jackie Onassis was reputed to have sold her clothes on consignment. I thought my mother would have been pleased at the company she was keeping.

The clothing, after all, was one of the pivotal ways in which my mother defined herself. She prided herself, quite rightly, on having a good eye. Her bedroom closets were filled from floor to ceiling with six decades' worth of high fashion. Silk, wool, fine cotton, leather, and suede were neatly arranged according to color and season. Plastic boxes displayed scarves; there must have been close to a thousand of them. Belts of every shape and size hung in a heavy tangle from some sort of contraption. When I tried to remove it, the whole thing crashed to the floor. The closets smelled like my mother: L'Air du Temps, coffee, a faint whiff of camphor.

I felt like a surgeon, cutting closer and closer to something essential as I went along. Who had she been? Why had all the stuff mattered to her so much? Were there clues? As I delved deeper into the closets, I slid a plastic box off a shelf and saw a Post-it stuck on top. Then I noticed that these Post-its were everywhere. Against the custom-made shelving, painted an eggshell white, they fluttered. Stuck to boxes, to the sides of garment bags.

White Anne Klein pants
Navy short-sleeved Calvin sweater
Hermes belt
Silk square scarf (Gucci?)

What were these? Packing lists? No, I realized—they were dreams, projections, fantasies of how life was going to be. In her good white pants and navy sweater, her perfect belt and jaunty scarf, my mother was going to be ... happy. Content. People would treat her as she *should* be treated: with admiration and even deference.

Black Armani jacket
Black skirt (Donna Karan?)
Sleeveless ivory silk blouse
Buccellati bracelet

In her spidery hand, she wrote out these lists, each time hoping it would be different. But it was never different. I would later discover, in her office, the stacks of unopened folders and notebooks purchased each year. If her wardrobe was a reflection of how she put herself together externally, my mother's office was a museum of unrealized ambition. The projects she was going to embark upon! The articles and books and screenplays she was going to write! As I pulled batches of notebooks still in their plastic wrappers from her office shelves, I imagined her annual trip to Staples, where she bought her supplies in bulk. I pictured my mother striding through the bright aisles purposefully, loading up her shopping cart with new folders and dividers and multicolored pens, a glimmer of an idea, a phrase, a concept, floating through her head like an aria. More Post-its, paper clips. This time—this time, she was really going to do it. She was going to write that book, that screenplay, that op-ed.

I packed up all the brand-new notebooks and folders in a box to give to Goodwill. I would never use them myself. They seemed cursed to me, even though I knew better. As I packed, I thought of the way my mother must have felt as she had placed each note-book carefully on top of those from the previous years: excited, inspired, full of big plans. These must have been some of her most hopeful hours.

81.

Steve Cope calls early meditation experiences *the noble failure*. The first time I heard him say it, I was reminded of my great friend and teacher, the late Jerome Badanes, who once said much the same about writing novels. *All novels are failures.* Even at the time, as a very young writer, I knew what Jerry meant. In novels—as in life—there is no perfection. We do the best we can with the tools we have at our disposal. Given that we are changing, the tools are changing, the thing itself is changing—there must be a moment when we stop. When we say, This is the best I can do for now. And though Jerry didn't apply the word *noble* to the failure of novel-writing, I think he would have agreed that there is nobility in the effort, courage in the dailiness—the *doggedness.* It is a process of trying and failing. Of beginning again.

These days, when I practice yoga and do sitting meditation, I am more aware than ever of the monkey that is my mind. Watch it go! One minute, I'm right here counting my breath, and I think I've got it—and the next, I've left the room, the house, the state of Connecticut. I'm in Italy, perhaps. Thinking about the teaching I'll be doing next month. I'm in New York, at last week's party, wondering if I said the wrong thing. *Come back,* I'll tell myself. This is the magic moment that Sharon Salzberg talks about. Not when your thoughts have wandered, but when you realize your thoughts have wandered. *Come back.* Gently, with compassion for the self, and its poor little monkey mind destined to fail.

82.

We discovered that I was pregnant the fall after my mother died. We had been trying—or maybe it would be more accurate to say that we hadn't been not trying. I was forty. Well, forty and a half. Half years had become important in matters of midlife fertility. We were squeaking in right under the wire. Blessedly avoiding the nightmare I had seen so many of my friends go through: the doctors, tests, labs, drugs, invasive procedures so often ending in heartbreak. I had *been through enough.* Did I think this—or is memory supplying it? Jacob's illness, my mother's death. The last few years had been rough. Didn't I deserve a break? Even though words like *deserve* really aren't part of my psychological makeup, still I wonder if there was a little bit of reverse hubris. A feeling that now—now things would be easier. I mean, God doesn't give us more than we can handle. And everything happens for a reason. Right?

My pregnancy felt *bashert*—the Yiddish word for "meant to be." There seemed a sad, poetic symmetry to it: the end of one life, the beginning of another. *You're breaking the cycle,* an old friend said. I knew what she meant. I had been an only child, and now I was going to be the mother of two children. The empty seat at our table would be filled. My ambivalence and fear had vanished. I was deeply, powerfully happy. I called my obstetrician, began taking prenatal vitamins, and made an appointment to see her in about a month. It seemed so right that I couldn't imagine anything going wrong.

At eleven weeks, Michael and I drove into the city to see the doctor. It was a beautiful, cloudless day. We held hands in the doctor's office, looked through well-worn issues of *Fit Pregnancy* and *Child*. I had my blood pressure measured, my weight. We joked with the nurses. I felt no worry, no pang of apprehension. Was it the hormones? I lay on the examining table and waited.

There are times in my life when all I can remember is Michael's face. I remember Michael's face the moment that Jacob was born; when the pediatric neurologist gave us the news; when he told me my mother was dead; and in the obstetrician's office, when she couldn't find the heartbeat. As I lay on the table, the wand of the sonogram pressed to my lower belly, I watched Michael's face. He watched the doctor's face. And that soft, caved-in expression—a magnitude of vulnerability—came over him once again.

"I'm sorry," she said.

"Isn't it possible that it's still too early?" Michael asked.

"I'm going to send you for a higher-resolution sonogram."

That afternoon, the machine at another doctor's midtown office detected the faintest of heartbeats. I saw it on the screen, flickering like a distant star. Bed rest for a week was suggested. Bed rest, and then we'd go back in for another look.

"Maybe it will be okay," Michael said as we drove back to Connecticut. "Maybe we miscalculated and you're not as far along as we thought."

I was mute as we sped along. The hollows of my eyes burned. I had hit up against the hard edge of something. I knew Michael was trying to comfort me—to comfort both of us—but I also knew that it was over. That faint, flickering star on the sonogram was burning out.

83.

I wasn't getting any closer to a personal relationship with God. It didn't occur to me to ask God questions, or to expect answers. We weren't really on speaking terms. To paraphrase Walt Whitman, I heard and beheld God in every object, yet understood God not in the least. And increasingly, that was okay. I didn't need to understand. Who was I, to understand?

One Saturday evening, Michael, Jacob, and I were at an outdoor party in Connecticut. It was a cold, drizzly night, and a huge bonfire was blazing in an open meadow. Dogs and kids were romping, and adults were huddled under shawls and blankets, warm by the fire. I stood shivering next to a woman I had gotten to know slightly—the mom from Jacob's school who I had first noticed all those years ago at the lake. The one whose son had a long, Samson-like mane of hair. The boy's hair had since been cut.

She and I were drawn into an instantly intense conversation—the only kind we ever had. Perhaps because we had both almost lost our children, we never made small talk with each other. I wondered out loud how she had known it was time to cut her son's hair. How had she decided that she had fulfilled her bargain with God?

"God told me it was time," she said. Her face was lovely, lit by the orange glow of the bonfire.

What did she mean, *God told her?* Was there some sort of sign?

"I got on my knees and asked God what to do, and he said that it was all right—it was time, now."

I looked at her hard. She was a bright woman, sophisticated, well-traveled. Nobody's fool. How could she believe God spoke to her? Maybe God *did* speak to her. Maybe he just didn't speak to me.

I remembered a story my aunt Shirley had once told me. A famous Orthodox rabbi, Joseph Soloveitchik, paid his respects to my grandmother during her convalescence after a massive stroke following my grandfather's death. My grandmother had already lost use of the left side of her body, and had lost most of her ability to speak. But through Shirley, she managed to convey her question to the rabbi. Why, she wanted to know, would God visit such hardship on an ordinary woman? She understood the trials God inflicted on great men like Abraham and Isaac, but why on someone like herself? The rabbi's answer was this: *Mrs. Shapiro, do you realize what you're asking? You're asking to have a dialogue with God.*

I didn't think I wanted a dialogue with God. What I wanted was an awareness of him: the unspeakable beauty, in the words of Thomas Merton, of a heart within the heart of one's life. I was enormously comforted by the idea of that inner, glowing, invisible heart.

84.

Every once in a while, the darkness was too much. It had been quite some time since I had woken up in the middle of the night and into an abyss of terror. But here I was. It was two in the morning, and the monsters had crept their way out of the closet. Every thought led to bleakness and despair. Three in the morning. Then four. I tossed, turned. Got out of bed, went downstairs. Drank a Diet Coke. Came back upstairs. Turned on my computer. Read Internet headlines, went on Facebook. Scanned through the status updates of perfect strangers. Went back to bed. I couldn't soothe myself. I wanted to be a person who would make a comforting cup of tea, curl up in an easy chair with a soft blanket, read something helpful. Perhaps listen to some Chopin nocturnes. Ride out the storm. But if that person had been accessible to me, I wouldn't have been in the state I was in to begin with.

What had set it off? It was a random Sunday night—nothing special. In fact, we'd had a good, busy weekend: a sleepover for Jacob, some errands, an early dinner with friends. Michael had finished a screenplay he'd been working on for months. We'd all tucked in early. Now, my mind had become a flip book of the most painful, devastating thoughts and images. They went something like this:

Michael clutching his arm, collapsing.

Me in a doctor's office—the prognosis dire.

The two of us in a car, a truck speeding toward us in the wrong lane.

Our wills—we hadn't redone our wills.

Money was tight. We always gambled a bit on our future.

What if Michael couldn't sell his next screenplay?

Our house—we could lose the house.

The phone ringing. The school. A freak accident.

Or an allergic reaction. Or—

The what-ifs continued. I thought about waking Michael. I could hear him snoring in the other room. But I didn't want to ruin his night too. I tried the *metta* phrases: *May I be safe. May I be happy.* But the simple words, which I usually found centering, were slippery. I couldn't hold on to them. I felt as if I were scrambling up a muddy incline. There was nothing to grasp. Just handfuls of dirt. *May I be strong. Live with ease.*

My heart pounded in my ears. My chest and stomach felt tight. I couldn't breathe all the way in. Maybe I was having a heart attack. It wasn't unheard of, after all. I resisted the urge to look up symptoms of heart attack or stroke on the Internet. No good was going to come of that. I imagined an ambulance racing up our driveway, lights flashing in country darkness. How had I gotten here—again? All the yoga, meditation, learning. All the brilliant teachers, the searching, seeking, reading—all the goddamn *thinking*, and still there was this: the waiting out the night. Face-to-face with my absolute aloneness. With the certainty of change. With precisely the suffering of which the Buddha spoke. *We know only that our entire existence is forced into new paths and disrupted,* Heinrich Heine once wrote. *That new circumstances, new joys and new sorrows await us, and that the unknown has its uncanny attractions, alluring and at the same time anguishing.*

In the darkness of my house as my family lay sleeping, all I could feel was the anguish of the unknown. Its uncanny attractions seemed like a mirage that could only be made out in the light of day. *May I be safe,* I kept repeating until finally the sun began to rise. *May I be happy.* I thought of something Jack Kornfield had once said while teaching meditation, which had later been repeated to me by one of his students: *This too, this too, this too.*

85.

Along with thinking of my daily meditation experience as the noble failure, I also began to think of it as the daily reminder. Each day I unrolled my mat on my bedroom floor. I practiced yoga and watched random thoughts float like dust motes through my head. Even in physically challenging twists and inversions, I could be elsewhere, thinking. I started to keep lists of what I found myself thinking about. Usually, it was some combination of what had happened earlier that day, or the day before—or what was about to happen later. I recalled that bit of Ayurvedic philosophy that Steve had once shared with me: *Be careful what you surround yourself with, because you become what you surround yourself with.* When I was able to notice the contents of my mind, I saw exactly how true that turned out to be. If I had talked to our accountant, he was in there. If I had received an e-mail from a student, she was in there. If we had been at a dinner party the night before, the guests were in there.

What was cluttering my mind when I *wasn't* noticing? Sometimes, particularly while driving, I would realize with a jolt that I had covered many miles in my car without the slightest bit of awareness. The outside world was a blur. Where was I? I had no idea. Instead, I was lost in some story—usually a story that hadn't even happened. What was the use of that? Over time, I began to wonder whether these stories had anything in common. I knew that neural pathways in the brain deepen over time: anxiety creates more anxiety, depression more depression. Maybe these stories also created their own pathways. They seemed to be variations on a theme. But what was the theme?

During my retreat at Garrison, forced inward by the silence, I found some clarity. I saw that no matter where my mind went, it all boiled down to this: it kept comparing. *How am I doing?* it constantly asked. *Am I up or am I down? How do people see me? Does she like me? Does he think I'm smart?* I cared—I saw this—far too much. It was horrifying, in fact, to realize how much of my mental chatter involved either shoring myself up, or tearing myself down. *How am I doing?* Over and over again, my mind asked the question in one way or another.

The awareness that I was always comparing was hard to tolerate, particularly in the silence. Did other people do this? I looked around the meditation hall at the other participants. The woman with the curly hair who carried a pot of lip balm with her all the time—she probably didn't compare herself to other people. What about the young guy in the front row, wearing a yarmulke? It would never have crossed his mind.

As I took stock of the room, comparing even about comparing, Sylvia and Sharon were giving a dharma talk on the Brahma Viharas—Buddhism's four most central virtues: lovingkindness, compassion, sympathetic joy, and equanimity. The path to achieving these virtues was strewn with stumbling blocks, of course. These were called the far-enemies and near-enemies.

"The far-enemy of sympathetic joy is envy," said Sharon. "And the near-enemy is comparing."

My ears pricked up. The near-enemy of sympathetic joy was comparing? I hadn't paid much attention to sympathetic joy. I felt joy for other people—easily reveling in the happiness and success of others. So I hadn't really paid much attention to this Brahma Vihara. I figured I had it down.

"It's painful and unskillful to compare," Sharon said, "no matter what conclusion we draw. Comparing creates agitation in the mind."

I felt Sharon's words go through me like a shock. There was the lesson and the internalizing of the lesson all at once. *Comparison itself* was the problem. Whether I was up, or down, or sideways was incidental to the very act of comparison, which was agitating. I understood this to be absolutely true. I thought of how I felt when I compared myself—whatever the result. It was diminishing, slightly sickening. *Unskillful*, that perfect Buddhist term.

In the months following Garrison, I attempted greater skillfulness. I unrolled my mat and began the process of my daily reminder. Comparing? I tried to talk to myself kindly, something I had learned from Sylvia. *Don't do that, honey. Come back.* Lost in a story? *Come back, come back.* Where were my feet? Ah, right there. Beneath me on the ground. Where was my breath? It filled my lungs, whether or not I paid attention. Where was I? Held in the infinite arms of the present.

86.

Our basement is filled with dead people's stuff. Boxes line the walls, some of them still taped closed. Plastic bins contain college diplomas, award plaques, golf trophies. Sets of china, cut crystal.

The lifetime achievements of aunts, uncles, grandparents—what do you do with such things? Throwing them away is impossible. Recently Michael came upstairs from a foraging trip to the basement carrying a shoe box. Inside the box were several dozen tapes from different eras: regular-sized cassettes, microcassettes, even a size that I hadn't seen before, midway between the two. Accompanying these was a clunky tape recorder.

"What do you think these are?" I asked.

We examined them. Some had dates, written in my mother's hand.

"Maybe she taped her patients," Michael said.

Here I had an ethical dilemma. My mother had gone back to graduate school when I was in college, and had become a psychotherapist. I had never been able to imagine my mother as a therapist. She had been a terrible listener, only able to talk about herself. Her response to any story was, *That reminds me of when I . . .* I marveled at the fact that she had patients, and had occasionally wondered about them. While my mother was ill, the phone rang one day, and it was a young woman who identified herself as a patient. "You must be Dani," the young woman said. I was speechless. How did her patient know my name? "Your mother talked about you all the time."

"Well, there's only one way to find out." Michael put some new batteries into the odd-looking recording device that had been in the box, and plugged in a random tape.

First there was a hissing sound. I sat hunched over at our kitchen table, half hoping the tapes would continue this way: a vast, impassable emptiness. But then, as if from a great distance, the sound of my mother's voice became audible through the hiss.

"I don't know what to tell you, Penny. It was a terrible week-end. Just terrible."

My mother wasn't talking to a patient. *Penny*. A name dredged up from the depths of the past. I felt like I was going to be sick.

"Do you know who she's talking to?" Michael fiddled with the volume.

"Paul doesn't have any life in him," my mother went on. "He's nothing but a wet noodle. And Dani—she's eighteen years old, you'd think she'd—"

I reached over and pushed the off button. *Penny.*

In 1978, the film *An Unmarried Woman* was released, the story of a wealthy Upper East Side woman struggling to find herself in the wake of divorce. The tagline of the film read: *She laughs, she cries, she feels angry, she feels lonely, she feels guilty, she makes breakfast, she makes love, she makes do, she is strong, she is weak, she is brave, she is scared, she is . . . an unmarried woman.* In the film, the central character, played by Jill Clayburgh, goes into therapy. The fictional therapist in the film was played by a real therapist named Dr. Penelope Russianoff, who was already something of a celebrity, having written best-selling books such as *Why Do I Think I'm Nothing Without a Man?* and *When Will I Be Happy?*

My mother saw the film and pictured herself as the sophis-ticated, urbane character portrayed by Jill Clayburgh. She then sought out Penelope Russianoff based on her performance in the movie. An image came to mind: a tall, handsome woman with long gray hair, wearing a flowing caftan, an arm stacked with bangles. A sunny office furnished only with pillows on the floor.

"These are my mother's therapy sessions." I turned to Michael.

"Oh, my God."

"Exactly."

We both stared at the cassette recorder as if it might be a nuclear device. What was on those tapes? In the privacy of a therapist's office, had my mother found the courage to express something that she hadn't been able to share with my father or me? Maybe the key to my mother's psyche was on these tapes. Fear mingled with hope—and guilt. This seemed the ultimate violation of privacy. On the other hand, my mother knew the tapes existed. She knew she was dying. She'd had ample time to destroy them if she had wanted to.

"What do you want to do?" Michael asked.

My finger, as if of its own volition, hit the play button again.

"Dani couldn't find her driver's license," my mother was saying. "She's so immature. I had to drive her all the way to Trenton to get a new one."

It was very nearly unbearable, listening to my mother's voice. The way she said my name, she practically spit it out.

"I was *eighteen*," I said out loud. As if maybe my mother could hear me.

"Irene"—now here was Penny Russianoff—"Irene, you're a stunningly beautiful woman. You don't have to put up with this shit. You look incredible for your age. If you don't mind my asking, have you ever had a face-lift?"

Whaaat? I had met Penny once. She seemed a little New Agey to me, but not like a complete and total quack. Why was she talking about face-lifts?

I switched off the recorder again.

"It's too awful." I felt numb, floaty. "She really hated me. I

mean, I knew it. I knew all this. But still—hearing it like this—
and her therapist is an idiot—"

"You don't have to listen to any more of it," Michael said.

"No. I want to."

I picked another tape and stuck it into the machine. More
hissing. Then, a rambling description of a dinner party: the outfit
she had worn, the way her friend's living room was furnished,
the meal itself. What was the point? Her voice was reedy with
unhappiness, so tightly strung it seemed ready to snap, and yet
the content of what she was saying was utterly inane. Why had
my mother gone into therapy? Obviously she recognized her own
misery, but she didn't want to get to the root of it.

"If I were Penny, I would have fallen asleep," Michael said.

I switched off the tape player. Over the next months, whenever I felt strong enough, I would summon up my nerve and plug
in another one. My mother's stories sounded rehearsed, as if she
never lost sight of the tape recorder. Always, she saw herself as a
rare and exotic bird—Jill Clayburgh trapped in the suburbs. Penny's occasional responses to her seemed like a parody of a 1970s
feminist therapist: "Irene, this guy"—that would be my father—
"this guy sounds really depressed. What's a vibrant woman like
you doing with a depressed guy?"

I would listen for maybe five or ten minutes at a time. I still
haven't heard all of the tapes, and doubt I ever will. At a certain
point, I realized that there was nothing new to learn—and that
very nothingness was something more painful than the deepest,
darkest revelation might have been. My mother would remain,
as she had always been, a great source of sadness and confusion.
How could she have been my mother? How could I have been her

daughter? When we first found the tapes, I called a friend to tell her about our discovery. "I'm worried for you," she said. "I think you're going to find out that your mother had some sort of secret life." I didn't know how to explain to her how much I wished my mother had a secret life.

87.

I was having tea with one of my smartest friends when she asked me if I had arrived at an answer. Did I believe in God? I knew this friend was an atheist. She had been dubious about my search from the beginning. "Why," she wanted to know, "would you take on such a thing? I mean, is this something you've thought a lot about? You're not a religious scholar."

There's nothing trickier than trying to talk about personal belief. Add on top of that trying to talk about personal belief with a very smart atheist. But I had some things to say. And wasn't that the whole point, really? To opt back in? To form—if not an opinion—a set of feelings and instincts by which to live?

"I would say yes." I took a leap. "I believe in God more than I did a couple of years ago. But not the God of my childhood. Not a God who keeps score, and decides whether or not to inscribe me—or anybody else—in the book of life."

"So what exactly *do* you believe, then?" She sipped her tea and waited for a better answer. I wanted to tell her that *exactly* and *believe* don't belong in the same sentence.

"I believe that there is something connecting us," I said.

"Something that was here before we got here and will still be here after we're gone. I've begun to believe that all of our consciousnesses are bound up in that greater consciousness."

I looked at my friend for any sign of ridicule, but saw none. She was nodding.

"An animating presence," she said.

That was as good a word as any: *presence*. As in the opposite of absence. By training my thoughts and daily actions in the direction of an open-minded inquiry, what had emerged was a powerful sense of presence. It couldn't be touched, or apprehended, but nonetheless, when I released the hold of my mind and all its swirling stories, this was what I felt. Something—rather than nothing. While sitting in meditation or practicing yoga, the paradox was increasingly clear to me: emptiness led to fullness, nonthought to greater understanding.

"Where does Judaism fit into all this?" she asked.

"It doesn't fit in," I answered. "It just is. I'm Jewish. Michael's Jewish. Jacob's Jewish." I thought of Sylvia Boorstein's elegant phrase: *complicated with it*. We were complicated by our history, by the religion of our ancestors. There was beauty and wisdom and even solace in that. I no longer felt that I had to embrace it all— nor did I feel that I had to run away. I could take the bits and pieces that made sense to me, and incorporate them into the larger patchwork of our lives.

I reached into my handbag for the well-worn black notebook I carried with me everywhere, writing in it only passages I had come across that had great meaning to me. "This is the way I've come to think of it," I said, turning the pages. The wisdom of a Catholic monk: "Here—from Thomas Merton. 'Your brightness is my darkness. I know nothing of you and, by myself, cannot even imagine how to go about knowing you. If I imagine you, I am mistaken. If I understand you, I am deluded. If I am conscious and certain I know you, I am crazy. The darkness is enough.' "

88.

It was hard to trust that everything really was okay. I knew what we had been told. The infantile spasms were infantile in nature. The medication had suppressed them. There was no reason to believe that they'd resume, or morph into something else. These seizures weren't a lifelong condition, but rather a brief and fiery storm that we had been able to douse before it burned us all to the ground. But still—I quietly worried. I *zorged*—a Yiddish word I later learned from Sylvia—which means "to create unnecessary anguish." We had been through the necessary anguish. Why was I still doing this to myself?

Jacob was three, then four, then five. He caught up to his peers. Almost no one in our new Connecticut life knew about his history. I was fierce, and fiercely private, about Jacob. He was thriving. Funny, smart, quirky, gorgeous. I choked back the tears I felt coming on when I watched him with a group of kids, kicking around a soccer ball, or singing in a chorus. But still—I couldn't quite let go. Letting go, it seemed, was an invitation for disaster to strike. Once, in *shavasana* at the end of a yoga class, I was in a state of deep relaxation when a woman who had been in a headstand behind me fell over backward, her feet landing hard on my chest.

As I jolted upward, the feeling I remember wasn't anger, or fear. It was akin to grief. *See? This is what happens when I trust that all is well.*

Vigilance was essential. Vigilance was the only answer in the face of all that could possibly go wrong. Wasn't it? I tried to make sure that my anxiety didn't rub off on Jacob, but I'm sure it did. To this day, he watches me carefully, assessing my mood. *What?* he'll ask. *What's wrong?*

One day, when he was in kindergarten, I came to school to pick him up and saw that he was doing something funny with his head. A fast kind of nodding that looked involuntary. I felt it then—the other shoe dropping. Were his eyes flickering? Was I imagining the whole thing? When we got home, I called his pediatrician in New York. She suggested I take Jacob for a second opinion, and gave me a name that was familiar to me from a few years earlier, when I carried a list of national experts around with me like a Bible.

A few weeks later, Michael and I drove into New York with Jacob, and went to the hospital where the doctor worked. The whole way in, I wondered if this was overkill. I hadn't seen the fast nodding again. There was no sign of anything wrong. Why subject Jacob to the poking and prodding of a stranger? My hypervigilance had once been very useful—it had saved Jacob's life when I first noticed the tiny seizures and rushed him to the neurologist. But when was enough enough?

In his office, the doctor checked Jacob's reflexes, tossed him a ball, asked him to write his name. He made notes about large and small motor functions. He looked into Jacob's eyes with a pinpoint flashlight. All the while, he chatted with Jacob about kindergarten, asked what sports he liked to play.

When he was finished with the exam, he set down his clipboard. "Do you know how lucky you are?" he asked me.

Yes. I knew how lucky we were.

But then the doctor hesitated. "This is probably unnecessary, but as long as you're here, why don't we do an EEG on Jacob. Just to be sure."

It had been nearly four years since Jacob last had an EEG. As a baby, he'd had more than I could count. Either Michael or I would cradle him as a technician applied cold, sticky goo all over his head, and then stuck a series of electrodes on top. The stuff had a sharp, chemical smell. He would cry and cry as he drank down a bottle of milk. He had to fall asleep before the test could commence. Now that he was a five-year-old, we had some explaining to do. A bottle of milk wasn't going to do the trick. We promised ice cream afterward, and a trip to a toy store. With every ounce of limited acting skill I possessed, I told him it was no big deal. We needed a picture of his brain. He needed to lie still for a little while. That's all.

As the goo was spread across his head, I wondered if he remembered the smell. Whether buried inside of him, there was a memory of the narrow room, the cold, sticky stuff, his parents holding him. The fear I tried not to let him see in my eyes. Now, in his Red Sox shirt and blue jeans, he lay there quietly as I held his hand. I hadn't bargained on this. It hadn't occurred to me that the doctor might order an EEG. This wasn't simply a second opinion. Now we were in the realm of quantifiable results. Peaks and valleys on an EEG strip. Suddenly, I was terrified.

Afterward, we sat in the waiting area while the results were read. Ten minutes went by, then twenty. Breathing was difficult.

Michael and I flipped aimlessly through old copies of *Newsweek*, watched Jacob play with the requisite train set that always seemed to be in these offices. His hair was matted down, making him look older.

The doctor finally emerged from his office and strode over to us, smiling.

"A normal result," he said. I could see on his face how rarely he got to say this to anxious parents. "A perfectly normal result."

89.

Sometimes I check my e-mail while driving.

I forget to wear my seat belt.

When in New York, I dash across the street during any break in traffic.

I used to smoke cigarettes, though I'm not sure that counts. I quit at twenty-five.

This is a list of actions—potentially damaging, even devastating actions—I do or don't undertake that are within my control. It's hardly like I'm skydiving, or helicopter skiing. A risk-taker I'm not. But I certainly don't need to check e-mail while driving. Obviously, I could be wearing my seat belt at all times. Jaywalking isn't really necessary. So why do it?

Last year, I was rushing to make a noodle kugel for Rosh Hashanah. I didn't bother to unplug the handheld electric mixer before I used my index finger to remove cheese that was stuck to the blade. I accidentally switched on the mixer and cut a gash into my finger. Michael saw it happening, and started to yell—*What did you do? What did you just do?*—as he reached the phone to call 911. It's the one and only time an ambulance has come up our driveway—despite all my nightmares and fantasies—and it was because of something I did that was entirely my fault.

Jacob's longtime babysitter, Maria, is a devout Mormon, and one of the most capable people I've ever known. She once told me that her religion teaches its adherents to focus only on the task at hand. When cooking dinner, cook dinner. When driving, simply drive. Whether walking, eating, arranging flowers, or putting a child to bed, do so with undivided attention. When making a noodle kugel, don't have your head in one place, and your . . . finger, say, in another.

I worry constantly about all those things that I can't control. Nutty stuff—but it's part of my fretting nature. In the words of Sylvia, I am easily startled. In the absence of anything to startle me, I am capable of startling myself. But when it comes to the things that are within my grasp, I am slowly learning what the Mormons—and the Buddhists, for that matter—already know.

One afternoon at Garrison, Sharon Salzberg spoke about a Buddhist teacher in India, a widowed woman with many, many children who had no time to sit on a cushion, meditating. How had she done it, then? Sharon had once asked her. How had she achieved her remarkable ability to live in the present?

The answer was simply this: she stirred the rice mindfully.

90.

I was blessed—or was it cursed?—with a highly attuned sense of my physical self, and could usually tell within days when I was pregnant. After the first loss there were others. These pregnancies lasted a few weeks, a month. One held on for nine weeks before I began bleeding. We lived with an absence, a ghost child. We didn't make travel plans. I declined out-of-town speaking engagements. My life was a split screen. Were we going to remain a family of three? Or was Jacob going to have the little brother or sister he often asked for?

We kept Jacob's baby clothes boxed up in the basement, along with his crib and bouncy seat. We stored his tricycle in the garage. We didn't decorate the spare bedroom, nor did we give it a name. It wasn't the guest room. It was the future baby's room, though we didn't call it that either. Jacob turned five, then six. It was beginning to feel like it was now or never. I was forty-two and a half, then forty-three. Conceiving the old-fashioned way had begun to be, statistically speaking, highly improbable.

One day while driving near my house, I had what felt like a eureka moment. I had the answer! My body was clearly defective. I secretly believed that I was to blame for Jacob's infantile spasms. No matter how the doctors had reassured me, I couldn't shake the feeling that I hadn't been able to protect him. What made me think it would be any different with another child? I knew—I was certain of this—what we needed to do.

I came home and told Michael my great idea: we needed to find an egg donor. A young woman with healthy eggs. Up until that moment, I had never considered the possibility, but now it seemed like the only way.

"An egg donor?" Michael asked. He looked concerned. "I don't know, honey. I'm not sure how you'll feel if—"

"It's fine," I answered, as if I had thought the whole thing through. "I love you, and the baby will be biologically yours. And Jacob will have a sibling. That's what matters."

Once I had arrived at this solution, it was as if I had leapt onto a fast-moving train. Though Michael remained unconvinced, he was willing to make the leap with me. What we wanted—a second child—overrode all possible misgivings. We had been pretty beaten down by the compounding losses, and it didn't take much to talk ourselves into it. We didn't stop to think—because stopping and thinking might mean stopping entirely. The key word was *want*. We *wanted*. And that desire made us blind and slightly crazy.

I embarked on a search for an egg donor with all the energy I could muster. Project Baby! I was good at projects. I did research, made lists. There were agencies, I quickly learned. Did I want a beautiful egg? An Ivy-educated one? A triathlete? Jewish? As if browsing the aisles of the world's most esoteric supermarket, the choices were staggering. There were supermodel eggs. Supermodel/genius IQ eggs. Supermodel/genius IQ/cello prodigy eggs. It was only a matter of deciding what was important to us.

Most evenings, after Jacob was asleep, Michael and I sat on the leather sofa in our library, scrolling through postage-stamp-sized pictures of donors.

"What about her?" I asked, pointing to a cute girl with curly brown hair. She played varsity tennis at a school I admired, and seemed like someone who might, in other circumstances, have been my friend.

"She's too tall," Michael said. "We're not a tall family." Then he pointed to a small blonde who looked a little like me. "What about her?"

I studied her photo and the biographical information next to it.

"She lists scrapbooking as her hobby."

"So?"

"I hate scrapbooking."

He rubbed the bridge of his nose, then looked at me.

"Does that matter?"

The thing was this: it did matter. *Everything* mattered. Height, eye color, intelligence, smile, hobbies, ethnicity, religion. Parents, siblings, grandparents. It mattered because I was trying to find my own replacement. At first, I thought maybe I could improve on myself—pick a prettier, smarter, less neurotic version of me. But as time wore on, I began to realize that I was looking for something else—something ineffable, and far harder to come by. I was searching for nothing less than a soul mate. I studied the results of highly detailed questionnaires—taste in food, age at first menstruation, musical preferences—as if these details, once added up, could possibly give me a real sense of the whole person.

I wanted—needed—to fall in love. But I couldn't fall in love. Not with a series of photographs, not with a list of personality traits. I began to feel older, more tired and more sad with each passing day. I had come face-to-face with something I wanted badly that I simply couldn't have. Finally, I had my second eureka moment, but this time it didn't arise from that intense wanting. Instead, it came from a place closer to the core. *This is my life*, was how it went. *My singular, blessed, imperfect, beautiful life.*

91.

I have practiced yoga with many different teachers since walking into my first class nearly twenty years ago. I've been to classes in Manhattan, Brooklyn, Long Island, Los Angeles, Boston, all over Connecticut. Crowded, sweaty classes where the mats overlap on the floor and from side angle pose, you can carefully study the intricacies of your neighbor's tattoo. Empty, air-conditioned studios with custom-colored mats and complimentary green tea served afterward. Once, from the carpeted locker room of such a studio on the Upper East Side, I heard a crowd cheering and rushed to the window just in time to see the Dalai Lama emerge with his entourage from a hotel across the street.

All of my teachers—some of whom I've never met, others who have become my friends—have taught me lessons I've needed to learn. I never know when a piece of wisdom is going to stick. I only know that, if I stay open and receptive, eventually I hear something new—or perhaps simply in a new way. From a teacher in Sag Harbor, I discovered the centering power of breath practice, *pranayama*. A teacher in New Orleans taught me to let my yoga practice settle in while lying in *shavasana*, rather than jump right into the rest of my day. Another—one I've never laid eyes on but whose podcasts are available on the Internet—had helpful insights into headstand.

But it was a teacher in Santa Monica who provided me one of my most valuable lessons. I had wandered into her class one morning, while on a trip to L.A. to meet with a potential egg donor. I was feeling confused and vulnerable. As soon as I entered the studio, I wanted to turn around and walk right back out. It was a cavernous room, filled with tan and impossibly fit twenty-something actor types wearing the latest yoga gear. The teacher—a tall, curvy woman named Ally Hamilton—paced the room wearing a cordless headset. I panted and sweated my way through the most physically challenging class I'd ever done, all the while thinking *I should leave, I should leave, I should leave.* But I didn't leave. And at the end of class, after *shavasana*, Ally instructed us in a practice that has since become a part of my everyday life.

At the end of my hour of yoga, after the sun salutations and twists and inversions and backbends and stretches, after I have rested for at least a few moments in *shavasana*, I sit up at the edge of my mat and place my palms together as Ally Hamilton did that morning in her busy California studio. I lift my palms to the center of my forehead—my third eye—and ask for clarity of thought. I wait until the idea of it has sunk in just a little bit. These things take time. Then I slide my palms down to my lips, and ask for clarity of speech. Again, I wait. Often, the phrase *Say what you mean and mean what you say* floats through my head. Finally, I slide my palms down to my chest, for clarity of action. I wait until I think I understand.

Clarity of thought.

Clarity of speech.
Clarity of action.

So simple, isn't it? So simple, and yet so easy to forget. I place my hands together in prayer and remember. Just as my father laid tefillin each morning, now I am finding my own touchstone. It may be different from my father's, but still, it's a ritual. I think he might even have approved. After all, it's a formal way of considering, however briefly, what matters most.

92.

It was a hot summer Sunday. Michael and Jacob were off to another Red Sox game, and I had planned to spend a relaxed afternoon with my aunt Shirley. I had been looking forward to some quiet time with her. As always, I was brimming with questions. But as she ushered me through her front door, she seemed a bit distracted.

"Sweetheart, I have a surprise for you. We're going to a wedding," she said. A wedding? I looked down at myself: I was wearing jeans, a T-shirt, flip-flops. I thought perhaps I had misheard her.

"I didn't tell you before, because I was afraid you wouldn't come," Shirley said. "Naomi—Joanne's youngest—is getting married today. In Chicago. Here, sit down. I'll be just a few minutes."

I watched as Shirley climbed up the wide, curved staircase, past Moe's electric chair lift. I had no idea what was going on. A wedding. In Chicago. I stood and walked around the library, looking at the assortment of family photos arranged on top of the grand piano. More children had been born since the last time I had visited. More young men in black hats, lovely wives holding newborns. My latest novel still had a place of honor on the coffee table. I gazed up at my grandfather's portrait, wishing for the thousandth time that I had known him.

"All right, this is the best I can do," Shirley called as she walked quickly back downstairs. She had changed into an elegant black suit, and was fastening a pearl choker behind her neck. "Cheryl is going to be here in a few minutes to set it all up."

"What's—I don't—"

The doorbell rang, and in came a young woman I recognized from various weddings and bar mitzvahs. She was the wife of one of my cousin Henry's sons, but I didn't know which one. She had four children in tow. The boys, who were perhaps three and four, were wearing suits and ties, shiny black shoes. The girls, slightly older, were in party dresses and Mary Janes. Everyone except for me seemed to be prepared for a special occasion.

"Bruno has Uncle Moe ready upstairs," Shirley said. "Come."

I followed Shirley and her great-grandchildren up to the master bedroom. Moe was in a wheelchair, wearing black trousers and a white business shirt. A yarmulke rested on top of his thin gray hair. Bruno, his home health aide, stood behind him. In the center of the bedroom, a very large computer monitor had been set up on a rolling cart.

"This should work," Cheryl said as she turned on the computer. "I tested all the equipment yesterday." With a few keystrokes, the screen was suddenly filled with a crowded ballroom. Hundreds of chairs were set up on either side of an aisle bedecked with white satin ribbons. In the front of the ballroom, a chuppah.

"See?" Shirley turned to me. "I told you we were going to a wedding."

Someone—probably Cheryl's husband—was holding a laptop on the other end, slowly panning the room. Video-chatting.

"Will you look at that." Shirley smiled. "Moe—Moe, can you see?"

My uncle's eyes were glued to the screen.

The faces of an older couple appeared.

"Moe? Shirley? Is that you?"

"It's us," Shirley called out.

"Mazel tov! We wish you were here!"

"This is as close as we could get," Shirley said.

The screen then filled with my cousin Mordechai. His black hat, long dark beard, twinkling brown eyes.

"Hi, Mom! Hi, Dad!" He then peered closer. "Wait a minute—is that Dani?"

I waved from behind Moe's wheelchair. Once again, inappropriately dressed for a family function.

The ceremony was beginning. Through the shaky, handheld laptop connecting the ballroom in Chicago to the bedroom in Brookline, we watched as the groom walked down the aisle, flanked by his parents. He wore a black hat and a black overcoat, which he had wrapped around himself. Underneath the overcoat, I knew, was a *kittel*, a shroud just like the one in which he would someday be buried. He looked like a character in a nineteenth-century novel.

"He's a psychoanalyst," Shirley whispered.

The groom had reached the chuppah. He turned to face the screen. *Mazel tov*, he mouthed. *Mazel tov*.

Naomi was now walking down the aisle, her parents on either side of her. She took her place next to her husband-to-be, then smiled and gave a small wave to her grandparents.

"She's a wonderful, very special person," Shirley said. "A beautiful bride."

We watched as the *sheva brachot*—the seven marriage blessings—were recited, each by a different rabbi. Naomi circled the groom seven times, her face serene beneath her veil. Shirley held Moe's hand. The great-grandchildren sat on the floor next to his wheelchair. Were those tears in my uncle's eyes? I couldn't tell.

In just a few minutes, the ceremony concluded with the breaking of the glass, and more calls of "Mazel tov!" from the wedding guests. But before the new husband and wife even looked at each other, before they embraced their parents or walked back up the aisle, they both turned to the laptop screen and spoke to the grandparents—the ninety-three-year-old man and eighty-six-year-old woman who were simply too old and frail to have possibly made the trip from Boston to Chicago.

"Mazel tov, Gram!" Naomi called. "Mazel tov, Grampa!"

"Mazel tov, sweetheart!" Shirley called. "Mazel tov, Meyer!"

In Chicago, the wedding guests began to dance. The women danced with women, and the men danced with men, in ever-widening circles. And in Brookline, Shirley reached her hands out to Cheryl, to her great-granddaughters, and to me. She was regal, incandescent as we danced around Moe's wheelchair—our circle connecting to that hotel ballroom and far beyond.

93.

Michael's parents are getting old. His father's eightieth birthday is coming up, and his mother just turned seventy-seven. They've been together for fifty-four years, and their marriage is one of the happiest I know. Partners in everything—they started their own real estate business together at their kitchen table and grew it into a sizable firm—they've hardly ever spent a night apart.

Like most couples, my in-laws have their own narrative: a story they've told themselves about how the rest of their life together is going to play out, based on what's come before. In this story, if one of them is going to suffer from poor health, it will be my father-in-law. Overweight, diabetic, he smokes cigars and eats foie gras. He enjoys a good scotch. Last year, his blood pressure dropped so precipitously that by the time he got to the hospital, the doctors didn't know how he could possibly still be conscious—much less have driven himself to the emergency room in his own car.

But it turns out that my mother-in-law—fit, slim, highly independent—is the one who is frail. She's been in and out of the hospital numerous times recently. Her condition is delicate. Her arrhythmic heart, it seems, is not cooperating with the narrative of their marriage. Now, she's the one who needs taking care of. Neither of them had been expecting this.

We talk on the phone most Sunday nights. These days—since a recent episode in Florida in which she passed out, injuring her knee in the process—I can hear the frustration in her voice. "Bill won't let me out of his sight," she says. "I can't even go to the bathroom by myself." I think of my father-in-law, who is gruff at the best of times, and how frightened and bewildered he must be. This wasn't what he had in mind. He was living one story, and suddenly he found himself in another. It's a lot to ask of an eighty-year-old man. It's a lot to ask of any of us—and yet this is what happens, again and again.

We are always adapting to new circumstances. We think we've found an answer that we can carry with us for our whole lives—and then it turns out that the questions themselves have changed. We think we've hit on something that will ease our suffering, or protect us—a talisman, a ritual, a form of prayer—and if we are honest with ourselves, even these keep changing.

When I first learned the *metta* phrases from Sylvia, they went like this:

May I feel protected and safe.

May I feel contented and pleased.

May my physical body support me with strength.

May my life unfold smoothly with ease.

A year later, at Garrison, I realized she had altered them. The original phrases she taught at Kripalu were musical, melodic, complex. I had been quite attached to the language, which absorbed and occupied my mind. Now, the phrases Sylvia taught were starker. Less musical. She used fewer words. At first, I didn't like them as much, and was slightly resentful that she had rewritten them. After all, why mess with a good thing?

May I be safe.

May I be happy.

May I be strong.

May I live with ease.

I recently asked Sylvia why she had simplified the *metta* phrases.
I knew there had to be a reason. She smiled at me, then beyond
me, as if looking over my shoulder into the distance. She nodded,
as she often did before formulating a response.

"I wanted something I would always be able to say—in old
age, in sickness—and have it be realistic," she said. "No matter
what happens, I can always wish for strength."

I thought, then, of the first words I had ever heard Sylvia
speak: *The whole world is a lesson in what's true.* The whole world is a
lesson—and the lesson keeps changing.

94.

Any place can become a sanctuary. Some of my most revealing
moments have taken place in unlikely spots: the church basements
where I attended AA meetings in my twenties; a particular bend
in the road near our house where the sky opens up at the top of
a ridge; an apple orchard in our town where the carefully pruned
skeletons of trees can be seen stretching over the gentle hills and
into the horizon. These are places that have made my heart soar,
which is the closest thing I understand to a sacred experience. But
is it necessary to have a more formal setting—a temple, church,
mosque, *zendo*—where prayer might be possible?

I received a call from a man who is the director of a therapeutic boarding school a few miles from us. I had vaguely known the
school was there—I noticed a discreet sign on the side of a road

I drive every day—but I hadn't really given it much thought. But now the director was calling to invite me to pay a visit. It turned out that he had read my novel *Family History,* part of which is set in an imaginary therapeutic boarding school, and while he had liked the book, he felt that I had portrayed a harsher environment than the one at his school. He wanted to give me a tour.

One blustery winter afternoon, I drove down the hill to the school, which is nestled into a glen tucked behind the main road. I parked in the visitors' lot, then walked past what looked like the main house—a restored New England farmstead—to the administration building. The director introduced me to a few of his colleagues, then began to show me around the campus. We walked through one of the dorms, then a few classrooms. The school seemed like a caring place, warm and serious. A place to get well. As we carefully traversed the icy paths, we talked about what I might do for them. Maybe come in and give a writing class to some of the adolescent girls?

We stopped, then, at a plain wooden structure, different from all the others. It was almost Amish in the simplicity of its design.

"This is our newest addition," the director said. "We've just built a chapel."

I climbed the wooden steps to the austere interior of the chapel. It was freezing inside, the wind whipping through it. I figured they must not be done building yet. The chapel itself was empty of furnishing, save for a low bench that ran around the perimeter of the room. The late-afternoon sun cast its last light across the floorboards. I stood in the center of the chapel and breathed in deeply. The air still smelled of new wood, but there was something else. A surprising scent. It took me a moment to realize that the chapel was a hayloft.

They *were* done building. The walls didn't meet the floor. The wind whipping through had been intentional. The smell of hay, of barn life. Nature would always be present in this space. The interior and exterior worlds seamless, existing in concert. I had an image, then, of my father's casket at his funeral. That simple, plain pine box. Meant to fall apart in the ground. *Dust to dust.* I took another deep breath. I was a little choked up, and tried to get a grip on myself. I didn't want to cry in front of the director. What was it about this place? It felt . . . sacred. Just standing there felt like a form of prayer. Precisely because of its emptiness, it vibrated with all of life.

95.

Yes, I had begun to recognize sacred places when I stumbled upon them. I had developed rituals that put me in closer touch with another dimension. I was a more contented and most definitely saner person. Some of the is-this-all-there-is despondency had been replaced by a greater sense of connectedness to something larger than myself. But—there was still a big but. I knew that in one important regard I was failing my son. No matter where else I might glean wisdom, we were Jews. Complicated with our Judaism and needing to deal with it.

My search for a rabbi and a congregation—a place to belong as a Jew—continued. It probably would have been easier in New York, or at least this is what I told myself. In New York, we would have had hundreds of options: Orthodox, Conservative, Conservadox, Reconstructionist, Renewal, Reform. Towering synagogues that felt more like cathedrals, and homey shuls with rabbis who played guitar and sang Bob Dylan songs. There was something for everyone. You couldn't walk a block without tripping over a gifted rabbi. I heard stories from my friends in the city about wonderful congregations they had discovered in Park Slope, or on the Upper West Side. But given where we had chosen to set down roots, our choices were limited.

The modern white synagogue on the hill with its baseball-joke-cracking rabbi was out. So was the coalition where we had spent the High Holidays. Two members of the board had staged a coup, firing Tamara, the spiritual leader to whom I had felt a profound connection. In her place, they hired a retired rabbi who was a divisive figure. The phones were abuzz with gossip.

This all felt familiar. It was the petty, spiritually bankrupt *mishegas* of my childhood. Temple meant gossip. Temple meant small-minded politics. Temple had nothing to do with spiritual connection. If this was temple, I didn't want any part of it. What was the point in finding the Jews if they were people with whom we had nothing in common? I wasn't sure where this left us. We had only a few years until Jacob would be of bar mitzvah age. There had to be another way.

I called Burt for advice, and he pulled out his directory of rabbis. Who knew that there was a directory of rabbis? It turned out that in a small, run-down industrial city twenty miles from us—in a direction we normally had no reason to drive—there was a shul. The rabbi was an old seminary friend of Burt's.

I made an appointment to meet this rabbi. As I drove to the shul, I was full of trepidation. I passed the place several times before spotting it: a low, nondescript building set back from the street, across from a parking lot. I sat in my car for a few minutes, gathering my thoughts. That old feeling—alienation, futility— came roaring back. I wasn't going to fit in here. I didn't fit in anywhere. I was a yeshiva-educated, overly assimilated Jew who still dreamed and prayed in Hebrew but could no longer speak a word of it. My desire to belong to a shul was all tied up with my love of my father—but he was long gone. I was a yogi, a tentative Buddhist, a meditator, a mom searching for meaning. How could I possibly explain any of that to a rabbi?

With considerable effort, I got out of my car and walked up the uneven sidewalk to the front doors of the shul. Inside, there was a bulletin board, a raincoat hanging on a hook, a basket of yarmulkes. The place seemed empty. The lights weren't on. There was no receptionist. Maybe, I thought, the rabbi had forgotten our appointment. Maybe I could just leave.

Just then, a slim man wearing jeans and a polo shirt, a woven yarmulke on his salt-and-pepper hair, poked his head out of an office.

"Dani? Rick Eisenberg." He stuck out his hand.

We sat down in his simple, uncluttered office. He leaned back in his chair and folded his hands behind his head.

"So tell me. How do you know Burt?"

I told Rick about Torah study, and how Burt and I had become friends. I then tried—haltingly—to explain my recent attempts to find a place to call home. I told him about my family background. The move from New York. The modern white synagogue on the hill. The coalition.

"I feel like a lost Jew in Connecticut," I said. But even as I said this, I realized it wasn't the whole truth. By now I was fairly certain that I would have felt like a lost Jew no matter where I lived. *Complicated with it.*

As we talked, Rick explained his path to me—from presiding over a large congregation in suburban New Haven to a decision to go back to school for substance abuse training, to this place in his life: a part-time position at this little shul and a full-time position as a substance abuse counselor. He was easy to talk to, intellectually curious, nonjudgmental, welcoming.

"Let me show you around," he said. "And listen—I know it's my job to try to get you to join the congregation. But don't join. Just come to services. Bring your husband and son. One Friday night a month we have services and I play the guitar. Lots of Shlomo Carlebach. See how it feels."

The building was nothing to speak of: tired, worn, badly in need of updating. The Hebrew school was made up of a series of windowless rooms in the basement. The sanctuary itself was simple, with a plain bimah and windows overlooking the street. But as I walked through the shul, I felt something I had begun to give up on feeling. I could imagine sitting there with Michael and Jacob. I could imagine coming for the occasional Friday-night service. I felt like *myself*, here in this house of worship. My past, my present—my *samskaras*, my contradictions—I could bring it all with me and just simply belong.

96.

Sometimes when I'm sitting in meditation, my sense of my physical body falls away. I am inside my breath—the breath breathing me, as the yogis say—and I experience something close to pure consciousness. There is no inside me, no outside me. Just a mind perceiving. A mind at one with what it perceives.

Sitting cross-legged on my yoga mat, in the quiet of my bedroom, I face the windows overlooking the meadow, one or both of the dogs lying quietly on the rug nearby. My eyes are closed. For a few fleeting seconds there is nothing to grasp. Nothing to hold on to. How long does it last? Impossible to say. Thinking about it breaks it to bits, of course. Examining, wondering, noticing— all of these pierce the magic and bring me back to my same old self.

But increasingly, I am able to carry that feeling—that pure awareness—around with me. It exists. I have felt it. And even though I can't always touch it, I know it's there. If I sit often enough, without expectations, it pays a visit. All that is required is to be quiet and mindful. To fight off the urge to jump up, check e-mail, jot down that idea. To sneak a glance at the clock. Surely twenty minutes have gone by. Time to get back to work.

Buddhist teachers often use the word *cultivation*. They speak of cultivating awareness. Of cultivating a practice. The minutes add up, then the days, weeks, months, years. Something takes root, and invisibly flowers. Cultivation is defined as the process of fostering growth. As it relates to biology, it is the way in which an individual organism grows organically; an unfolding of events involved as an organism changes gradually from a simple to a more complex level.

97.

Jacob has just learned to ride a bicycle, and on weekends either Michael or I take him to the campus of his school, which has wide empty parking lots and gentle sloping hills. Jacob came a bit late to the skill of bike-riding, mostly because he didn't want to fall.

"You can't learn without falling," I told him. "I fell. Daddy fell. Everyone who ever learns how to ride a bike falls."

Where does he get this tendency? I fear he has inherited it from me—this feeling that everywhere lurks imminent danger. *The chain ganglia*, as the osteopath explained. *It's hereditary. You think you're under attack, even when nothing is there at all.*

Most weekends I sit in my car near the ice hockey rink, listening to NPR or reading a book, keeping half an eye on him as he makes bigger and bigger circles. He's gotten his balance now—no longer afraid of falling—and waves to me from a distance as he rides off, disappearing from view. He's gone from nervous to cocky in no time at all.

One, Mississippi, two, Mississippi, three, Mississippi. I notice how long it takes for him to come around the other side. I roll down my window, listening. *Four, Mississippi.* There he is, pedaling madly. Another few seconds and I would have driven around the side of the building to make sure he's okay.

He pulls up to the car, red-faced beneath his helmet, breathless.

"There's a jump down there, Mom. It's sick!"

He sounds like a teenager.

"Can I try it?"

"Oh, honey—you've only been riding for a—"

But then I stop myself. I think of all the ways I'm going to have to learn to take my eyes off him for more than a few minutes. The ways we're both going to have to learn to let go. Today it's a bike ride. Tomorrow, a sleepover. This summer, sleepaway camp. Every day there are small leaps of faith. He is no longer my baby with the storm in his brain. Which is only to say that now he's in no more danger than the rest of us.

He makes another circle. Disappearing, reappearing. Gliding up to me.

"Come on, Mom. Can I?"

I bite my tongue to stop from saying, *Be careful.* Instead, I reach out the car window and brush a sweaty lock of hair from his forehead.

"Sure, honey. Go for it."

98.

According to the legend, the Buddha was a man of twenty-nine when he left home in search of enlightenment. Until that point, he had been protected and nurtured by his adoring parents; he grew up surrounded by wealth, beautiful things, ease of life. But as he began to experience the pain of being human—impermanence, the inevitability of loss—he grew restless. He saw that beauty fades. Possessions disintegrate, given enough time. Love surely leads to suffering and grief. The Buddha—or Siddhartha Gautama, as he was then known—longed to join the ranks of homeless ascetics and monks who lived in the forest next to the Ganges River, all searching for what they called "the holy life."

The Buddha slipped away in the middle of the night—afraid to say good-bye to his wife lest she try to convince him to stay. After all, his infant son was only a few days old. But the Buddha wanted nothing to do with his child. In fact, he gave him the Pali name Rahula, which means "fetter."

This is how the Buddha and the spiritual seekers of his day saw the ties of domesticity. *Fetter*: to shackle, manacle, handcuff, clap in iron, put in chains. *Fetter*—a verb, an active thing: to restrict, restrain, hinder, hamper, impede, inhibit, curb, trammel. Or informally, to hog-tie. It was very clear. Having a family—loving and nurturing a family—was incompatible with a life of seeking.

Not much has changed, really, since the time of the Buddha. The monks had another word for all forms of attachment: *dust*. As in grime, filth, smut, soot, fine powder. To love is to have one's vision occluded. To live in the material world is to see life through a lens distorted by frail and tender human longings. Whether the Buddha and his forest monks or Merton's Christian hermit or Thoreau's journey to Walden to transact his private business with *the fewest possible obstacles*, those who seek the purest spiritual knowledge do so alone.

99.

The mezuzah we bought in Venice remained in the satin interior of its box for a very long time—so long that when I was finally ready to affix it to the doorpost of our house, I had no idea where it could possibly be. Michael and I combed the kitchen. We had left the box on the butcher-block counter for so many months that it almost seemed to belong there, with other accumulated stuff that had no proper place: Jacob's handmade ceramic tortilla chip bowl; an extra set of car keys. But now the mezuzah was missing. After hours of searching, Michael found it in the laundry closet, in a drawer full of spools of thread and a collection of hotel sewing kits.

Why had I been avoiding this? I mean, we had schlepped the mezuzah all the way home from Italy—it would seem it could have made the last leg of the trip from suitcase to doorpost. But I had been taking baby steps. Ambivalence, even laziness, played a part. But more than anything, it was the same paralysis that had visited me that day while we were in the Judaica store. How could I affix just a single mezuzah? What was the blessing? Where was the rabbi? There was a right way and a wrong way to do this, and instead of risking doing it wrong, I had done nothing at all.

Finally, I sent Burt an e-mail asking for help. I was secretly hoping he would offer to come over and do it himself—but it turns out that affixing a mezuzah doesn't require a rabbi, or even a screwdriver. Within moments, I had his response:

1. Affixed to the doorpost to your RIGHT as you enter; on the upper third of the upright doorpost. Upper side is to be tilted toward the inside of the house. If the doorpost is not wide enough for a diagonal tilt, affix Mezuzah upright.
2. Can be affixed with nails, glue, two-sided tape . . .
3. The brachah for affixing a Mezuzah:

Barukh Attah Adonai Eloheinu Melekh HaOlam, Asher Kiddshanu BeMitzvotav VeTzivanu Likboa Mezuzah.

So simple, really. I wondered why it had taken me so long to ask about the protocol. The early evening sky was a soft, dusty pink when Michael marked the spot on the kitchen doorpost and drilled two holes. I had printed out Burt's e-mail so we could say the blessing. Then I called Jacob away from his Red Sox game.

"Honey, come outside for a minute. We're putting up the mezuzah."

"What's a mezuzah?"

"Remember when we were in the Jewish ghetto in Venice? We went into that store?"

The three of us stood on the front porch. On one side of us, the remainder of a cord of wood. On the other, a weathered bench, a basket overflowing with balls and sports equipment. The dogs sat at attention, watching to see whether there was any fun in this for them.

I showed Jacob the filigreed silver, the openwork revealing scrolls inscribed with minuscule Hebrew lettering.

"All of that is handwritten," Michael said.

Jacob examined the mezuzah.

"Does it light up?" he asked.

"No."

"Does it do anything?"

"Well, no."

I could see he was disappointed, but nonetheless Jacob recited the transliterated blessing along with me. *Barukh Attah Adonai . . .*

Michael tightened the screws. I thought of what Burt had told me that day at the seminary: *They say if you wrap yourself in tefillin and place a mezuzah on your door, you're protected from harm.* He had paused then. His voice was wistful when he concluded, almost as an afterthought: *Would that it were so.*

I didn't think the mezuzah was going to protect us, any more than I had faith that the *metta* phrases offered any kind of specific immunity. I was pretty sure there was no parking-spot-procuring God, swooping down from on high, helping out in a crisis—or even a traffic jam. I wished I believed that—but I didn't. I simply didn't. Still, here was a form, a ritual, a fulfillment of an ancestral commandment. It was something, rather than nothing. Another daily reminder—right there on the doorpost of our house—to stop for a moment. To take a breath. To pay attention and listen well.

100.

Michael, Jacob, and I wandered through the cemetery looking for my mother's grave. It was a damp, foggy day; the rain had grown ever steadier during the drive from Connecticut to New Jersey, and was now pouring down on us. I held Jacob's hand and helped him over a puddle. The ground was muddy, rutted, our feet leaving deep impressions along the narrow pathways.

"There it is." Michael spotted a modest family tombstone engraved with my mother's maiden name, Rosenberg. She was buried here alongside her parents and sister, only a few miles away from the chicken farm where she had been raised. I hadn't remembered how close to the edge of the cemetery her grave was—right near the chain-link fence. In fact, I remembered very little about this place. I had been numb and somehow shocked the day of my mother's funeral, even though her death had not been a surprise.

Years had gone by. I had been afraid of coming back here. This fear masqueraded as indifference or even laziness, but deep down I knew it was more than that. The cemetery had written to inform me that her footstone had been installed, but I had never arranged for a proper unveiling. Who would come? Her brother, who had barely spoken to her in years? My father's family, from whom she had been estranged? With each passing anniversary of my mother's death, it seemed less likely that I would ever visit her grave. This felt like a failure on my part. What was I so afraid of?

I thought of the black crows pecking at my front yard. *There's Irene.* Did I feel like she could reach out and grab me from beyond the grave?

I walked over to her footstone and waited to feel something. I was here, now. I had finally felt strong enough to make this journey. "Whatever you think you can do or believe you can do, begin

it," Goethe once wrote. "Action has magic, grace and power in it."
Jacob stood very near me.

"That's where Grandma is buried," I said. "See the inscription?"

Jacob looked down. *Beloved and loving daughter, wife, sister, mother.*
Was it true? Had she been beloved—or loving?

"Someone has been here," Michael said. I noticed, then, that the
other footstones—my grandmother's, grandfather's, and aunt's—
all had small rocks and pebbles placed on top of them, as did
the larger family tombstone. Someone had visited, and observed
the Jewish tradition of leaving stones—a sign of permanence—
instead of flowers. Only my mother's grave was unadorned.

I bent down and pried a sand-colored rock from the wet
ground and handed it to Jacob. It was the size of the inside of
his fist.

"Do you want to put this on Grandma's grave? And maybe say
something quietly to yourself—like a prayer, or something you're
thinking?"

He walked over and with great dignity laid the rock next to
my mother's name.

We circled the footstones of his great-grandparents and great-
aunt, and I said their names out loud: *David Rosenberg, Anna Ruth
Rosenberg, Rosalyn Copelman.* He was having trouble keeping them
straight, and who could blame him? They were abstractions to
him. They were practically abstractions to me. I dug around for
more stones to leave behind.

I placed pebbles on each of their graves, still feeling nothing.
No longer afraid. No longer angry. We had driven three hours in

terrible weather to come here, and I was just going through the motions. My inability to feel anything felt like a defeat. I stared at the ground. Whatever physical remains of my mother were left in this world were right beneath me, and I couldn't muster a single tear.

The rain had turned torrential. Michael's shirt was soaked, and Jacob was shivering. His bright red Crocs were caked with dirt.

"Why don't you guys wait in the car? I'll just be a minute."

I watched the two of them stepping through mud and puddles on their way out of the cemetery. They walked back to the car parked on the other side of the chain-link fence, hazards flashing.

I stood near my mother's footstone. I didn't think I would ever come here again, and now I couldn't quite bring myself to leave. The rain beat down even harder. And then—though I hadn't planned on it and didn't know whether it was appropriate or might even be sacrilegious—I began to recite the Mourner's Kaddish.

Yitgadal v'yitkadash shmei rabah.

The tears came with the Hebrew words. *B'alma di v'ra khirutei v'yamlikh malkhutei.* I stumbled my way through the kaddish, hearing a chorus in my head. My father's voice, reciting it for his father. My grandfather and great-grandfather reciting it at the grave of my great-great-grandfather in the Polish shtetl. The candles that burned each Yom Kippur on our kitchen counter for my parents' dead parents, that now burn on my own kitchen counter: twin flames.

O'se shalom b'im'romav. I was crying hard now.

Beloved and loving daughter, wife, sister, mother.

She had been beloved. It was this I hadn't wanted to feel.

This—beneath the anger, the numbness, the fear. She was my mother, and I had loved her.

I turned away from her grave and walked back out the cemetery gates, back to the rest of my life. My husband and son were waiting for me.

101.

This morning I wrote a condolence note to an acquaintance—a mom of one of Jacob's friends—whose elderly father passed away. It is one of several such notes I've written this year. This is the natural order of things—the time of life we've now entered. *The afternoon,* as Jung called it. *Thoroughly unprepared we take the step into the afternoon of life.* Are we unprepared simply because preparation is not possible? It's hardly an exam we can bone up on. We learn—if we are lucky we learn—as we go.

Jung defined midlife as over the age of thirty-five. I know people who don't consider themselves middle-aged at fifty. It doesn't really matter, except in this regard: however we think of ourselves, we are in the center of the stream. Much has already happened, and has formed the shape of our lives as surely as water shapes rock. Much lies ahead of us. We can't see what's coming. We can't know it. All we have is our hope that all will be well, and our knowledge that it won't always be so. We live in the space between this hope and this knowledge. Every morning, when Michael and Jacob leave for the ten-minute drive to school, I call after them: *Drive carefully!* And Jacob calls back to me: *We will!* Is it a superstition? Perhaps. Do I believe it will make a difference? No. But still, I say it—because saying it is all I can do.

Two women I know—both in their forties—were diagnosed with serious cancer this year. They have kids Jacob's age. In an instant, their lives became about doctors and surgeries and chemotherapy and odds. The husband of a dear friend had testicular cancer and major surgery. The outlook is good for him. A woman in the Torah group lost her ten-year-old son to a rare form of brain cancer. Friends have had biopsies that have turned out to be nothing. A good friend is having twins. People my age have kids in preschool, kids off to boarding school, kids applying to college. Anniversaries have been celebrated. Trips taken. Jobs and retirement funds lost. Quite a few parents are ill. A number of parents, aunts, and uncles have died. There have been car crashes, heart attacks, falls. There have been phone calls piercing the night.

This too, this too, this too, Jack Kornfield said. Life keeps coming at us. Fleeing it is pointless, as is fighting. What I have begun to learn is that there is value in simply standing there—*this too*—whether the sun is shining, or the wind whipping all around.

102.

I sat cross-legged on my bedroom floor, trying to listen to my breath. *Inhale*, two, three, four. *Exhale*, two, three, four. I was having trouble concentrating. It had been a hard couple of days. My uncle Moe had died one morning as my cousin Henry was preparing him to lay tefillin, and even though Moe was ninety-three, even though he had been suffering and very ill for many years, still I was grieving.

At Moe's funeral near Boston the day before, hundreds of mourners filled the sanctuary. A succession of eminent rabbis gave eulogies. I learned things about Moe that I hadn't known before. He had been president of the Orthodox Union, and the authentication stamp on kosher food had been his idea. In a rapidly assimilating postwar America, he saw the need to circle the wagons in order to keep Orthodox customs alive. He had traveled the country in support of *mechitzot*—the partitions that keep men and women separate in shul.

I sat with Michael and Jacob in the rows reserved for relatives. In front of us, a familiar-looking young woman—a cousin?—rifled through a siddur affixed with dozens of brightly colored Post-its. Everyone except for us seemed to know what to say and do. We were alone—my little family—an isolated, rogue cell within the larger organism of Moe's family. I didn't mind, really. I was used to this particular discomfort. Before we got out of the car in front of the shul, Michael had turned to me, squeezing my hand: *Remember*, he said. *It's okay to feel like an outsider. You are an outsider.*

Thoughts clouded my mind as I tried to count the breath. What would Shirley do now? Would she stay in the vast, empty house in Brookline by herself? Would she move in with one of her children? Shirley was keeper of the flame, and her house contained within it everything that was left of my grandparents—of my father's childhood life. Now it would be further dispersed until, one day, it would disappear completely.

Inhale, two, three, four. *Exhale*, two, three, four. My mind stubbornly refused to quiet down. Jacob had wanted to attend the funeral—in fact, he insisted on it. He felt a sweet connection to Moe. *He's my family, Mom*, he said. Before we got to Boston, I tried to prepare him. I was nervous that the Orthodox funeral would be too much, but it didn't feel right to keep him away. He was right. They were his family—and I had so little to give him in that regard.

They believe in God differently than I do, I had told him. Feeling, at least, some comfort in being able to say that I believed in anything at all. But once in the sanctuary, watching my relatives as they entered the prescribed orchestrated rituals of mourning with an almost choreographed precision, it seemed to me that they had a lock on God. They had certainty. I would always have doubt. They had one set of rules and rituals; one rabbi after the next referred to *Torah-based Judaism*. They lived—literally—by the book. I lived by an eclectic array of rituals, by many different books. They had continued on the path set by my grandparents, digging deeper as they went. And I—Michael was right—I had chosen life on the outside. I was an outsider.

Counting the breath wasn't working. I kept seeing Moe's casket borne on the shoulders of my cousins—those same cousins who had carried my dead father more than twenty years earlier. Shirley standing, silent in the bitter cold as the casket was placed in the hearse. The line of the funeral procession as it began its long journey from Boston to JFK Airport, and then onto an El Al flight to Israel, where Moe would be laid to rest. I imagined the second, smaller service in the cargo hold before my uncle's remains were loaded onto the plane. My eighty-six-year-old aunt and four cousins boarding the flight, settling into their seats, prayer books in hand.

May you be safe. By now, they would have buried Moe at the cemetery near the gates to Jerusalem. *May you be happy.* They would be back on the plane, flying home to sit shivah. I hoped the trip wasn't too much for my aunt. *May you be strong.* I was no longer having trouble focusing now. *May you live with ease.* I sent the phrases—the wishes and hopes, my form of prayer—out into the invisible world.

Later that afternoon, Jacob came home from school and told me that during his school assembly he had raised his hand and asked if they would all say a prayer for Uncle Moe. Two hundred blue-blazered New England prep school children recited the Lord's Prayer. *Our father who art in Heaven.* A woman sat cross-legged on her bedroom floor practicing ancient Buddhist blessings. *May you be safe.* An elderly widow and her four grown children were airborne, bent over their siddurs as the sky outside their windows turned from night to day. *Yitgadal v'yitkadash.* Each of us human, full of longing, reaching out with our whole selves for something impossible to touch. Still, we are reaching, reaching.

acknowledgments

A small bookcase near the desk where I write is lined with books that I found inspiring. In addition to those I mention or quote, I was particularly helped by the following: *For the Time Being* by Annie Dillard; *The Buddha* by Karen Armstrong; *A Grief Observed* by C. S. Lewis; *Nothing to Be Frightened Of* by Julian Barnes; Pascal's *Pensées*; *Do You Believe? Conversations on God and Religion* by Antonio Monda; *Ambivalent Zen* by Lawrence Shainberg. I am also indebted to the works of Sharon Salzberg, Larry Rosenberg, and Jack Kornfield, and the poems of Jane Kenyon.

Stephen Cope, Sylvia Boorstein, and Burt Visotzky have been my shining lights on this journey. I didn't set out to find a yogi, a Buddhist, and a rabbi, and can only marvel that my initial, tentative questions led me to extraordinary thinkers who have now become such dear friends.

I am grateful to my early readers Jack Rosenthal and Jack Gilpin. Abigail Pogrebin—fellow sojourner, astute reader—talked me out of more than one tree. Mitchel Bleier shared his extensive knowledge of yoga philosophy and allowed me into his advanced yoga class even though I can't do a handstand in the middle of the room. Tracy Bleier and Ally Hamilton—goddesses both. Maria Da Silva made it possible for me to do what I needed to do.

My gratitude, as always, to my wonderful agent, Jennifer Rudolph Walsh, whose support I feel every day. Andy McNicol read early pages and offered a generous and spot-on critique. And my deepest thanks to my editor, Jennifer Barth, who got this book from minute one and has been this writer's dream.

My beloved aunt, Shirley Feuerstein, is simply the most graceful person I have ever known.

Finally, my two favorite men: my son, Jacob Maren, the beating heart of this book. And my husband, Michael Maren, who embodies the very essence of the word *devotion*.

About the author

About the book

Insights,
Interviews
& More . . .

Read on

A Conversation with Dani Shapiro

© Lorin Klaris

This interview was conducted by Kari Wethington and originally appeared in ELLE *magazine. Copyright © 2010 Hachette Filipacchi Media, U.S. Inc.*

IN DEVOTION (HARPER), bestselling memoirist and novelist (and *ELLE* contributing editor) Dani Shapiro (*Slow Motion, Family History, Black & White*) movingly unravels her personal history—from her Orthodox Jewish upbringing and her parents' seemingly unrewarding marriage to her near-nervous breakdown when her infant son suffers life-threatening seizures—and her subsequent quest to resolve a spiritual unease and to satisfy her son's questions about God.

Shapiro excavates her psyche to examine

the milestones of her life in the shadow of her religious past. She eloquently grasps at the eternal questions that pierce her deeply—What's our purpose? Who's listening?—raking up familial histories and dredging through the ephemera of her late parents' lives to make sense of her present.

Through yoga and meditation ("a formal way of considering, however briefly, what matters most"), Shapiro attempts to quell her restless mind, vexed as it is by both the mundane—sickness, car accidents, bills—and the thorny: Why did her mother, an atheist, choose to live life according to a faith she didn't believe in? As Shapiro struggles to reach higher ground, she begins to find that perhaps there's no ultimate escape. Rather, "Life keeps coming at us. Fleeing is pointless, as is fighting."

Shapiro's spiritual inquiry digs at doubts many of us face about our place in the universe, and her struggles with the God question serve as a hopeful reminder that a belief system can begin with an individual manifesto: less a set of rules than a matrix of bits and pieces that form the "patchwork of our lives."

ELLE: In *Devotion*'s opening scene, you're having a moment with an "energy worker," and you say what happens defies everything you believe—that you are on the "other side of logic." Do you think letting go of logic is a necessary part of the spiritual journey you take in this book?

Dani Shapiro: Yes, I think that essentially there's logic on one side, and really anything resembling faith is on the other ▶

> 66 Her struggles with the God question serve as a hopeful reminder that a belief system can begin with an individual manifesto. 99

side. Logic and faith don't occupy the same side. When I started writing *Devotion*, I entered it wanting to spend a couple of years living inside all the questions I had, and one of the things I realized when I was writing was that there are books that a writer undertakes because she wants to go on a journey, and there are journeys a writer undertakes because she wants to write a book. This was very much a journey I wanted to go on, and the only way I could really give myself the permission and the time to do it was by knowing that it was what I was doing for work, that I could spend two years cross-legged on my floor and feel like I was working. Otherwise I'm way too type A, and it would have felt both impossible and self-indulgent. I needed to slow down and quiet down deeply into a lot of these questions, yet at the same time what I was looking for, and continue to, is a way to have this exist within a regular, normal, modern life.

ELLE: For many women who are already juggling a career, relationships, and kids, how can this kind of spiritual assessment fit into their "normal, modern" lives? And in families, does this weight usually fall on the woman's shoulders?

DS: I think it's primarily women who begin to ask these questions. At least in my experience and for people I've talked to, the men don't just have greater resistance—they have less of a conscious need, and I say *conscious* very deliberately because it's a human need when it arises. It's not gender specific, but I do think it's women who tend to start having that sort of little whispering voice of "I want more here" and "I want more for my family." I was joking around with my son the other day because he was complaining about having to go to religious school on a Sunday morning, and he said, "Why do I have to go?" and I said, "Your father hated Hebrew school and he went, your father's father hated it and went." The fact is that most husbands, regardless of religion—it's an old-fashioned gender divide where the husband wants to stay home and the wife is the one who drags herself and her children to whatever spiritual center they're going to. My husband is an atheist, and at a certain point while I was writing *Devotion*, he turned to me and said, "I'm really glad you're doing this," and I think it has opened him up in ways he's very happy about but wouldn't have done himself. I don't care that I had to do it. It's good for the people that I love, but he wouldn't have done it on his own, for sure.

ELLE: Your son, Jacob, suffered from life-threatening infantile seizures. How did the experience of his illness affect your thoughts about religion and God? If that chapter of your life hadn't happened, would you have still taken this journey? What else could have spurred it on?

DS: I think there are a number of things that were seeds of this journey. One was certainly Jacob's illness and the feeling I had at the time of wanting desperately to believe in something and knowing I didn't particularly—also, the need to pray, even though I didn't know what or who I was praying to, but also I think if we were still living in New York, I wouldn't have written [*Devotion*]. There's something about urban life—you walk out your door, and you're in a steady stream of life happening around you, and it's very easy to get caught up in that stream and simply kind of keep on moving. I found when we moved to the country that the absence of that was so stark. I'd open my door, and instead of thousands of people walking by and horns honking and lights flashing and dogs being walked and shop windows and endless stimuli, what I was faced with was kind of nothing. What I was faced with was myself in a much starker and more profound way than I had ever experienced before. What was going on inside of me became louder because everything around me became quieter. And lastly, [there's a line] from Carl Jung—"thoroughly unprepared we take the step into the afternoon of life"—that was such a fundamental thing for me. Reading those words and recognizing them as absolutely true and wanting to be prepared, but not knowing how to do this next step. I was also reaching a point in my life where I wanted to reconcile myself or understand better the way I was raised, and my very religious childhood felt like a part of me that I had abandoned. Sometimes—it just happened to me the other day: I realized there was a tune running through my head, and so often the tune is something from my childhood, and often it is something I heard in temple. Even though I might not be able to translate the words, still there's attachment to them, the way we're attached to smells and sights and sounds and tastes. As a fiction writer, that's been a ▶

preoccupation of mine: Can you really just close the door and leave the past back there behind you, or is the door going to blow open at some point? I did want to feel like life's all of one piece.

ELLE: You say your life is "complicated with Jewishness." Was there ever a time you resented that? Do you think having that background helped or hurt your search for these truths?

DS: When I started the search, I didn't know how much of any one thing it would be. I was doing a lot of yoga and learning to meditate, and I found that extremely helpful, and still do and hopefully always will. I didn't know how much my years of being in therapy would play into it. I think growing up with something helped me. If we grew up with nothing, we're complicated with that. That's the thing I keep hearing from people. The friends of mine who have grown up with nothing have a longing for something but feel like they don't know where to begin. When I started meditating, even doing yoga, I felt like it was hard to allow myself to develop any other kind of practice [outside of Judaism], like I was somehow being untrue to my heritage, and that was something I had to get over and was probably the greatest revelation to me. I was very suspicious of the idea of answers. The people I met along the way who had thought the most about this stuff, and who I really admired, take a little bit from here and a little from there. They were able to glean bits of wisdom, and it struck me as a very modern idea. I had always thought of people who do that as being intellectually lazy and looking for solace, and that it wasn't pure, and that's part of where I come from, that there's a right and wrong way to do things. That hamstrung me in terms of feeling like I could find myself.

ELLE: What is your hope for Jacob as he gets older and faces similar questions? Do you think he'll have these same struggles?

DS: I hope for him that he will feel complicated at some point because what I feel now is that I'm giving him *something*. The whole book began with him asking me questions. I was uncomfortable with not having anything to say to him. I think Jacob is going to be complicated by being the son of two writers, by being sick as an infant, and by the fact that I've written about him in this book.

There have been moments for me—and they tended to be moments of great emotional intensity, moments of grief and mourning, but also of joy, deaths, the birth of my son, and my wedding day—when I was glad to have ritual. I was glad to know, *This is what we do in this moment, these are the steps that we take.* There is something, even though I didn't realize it [at the time], comforting to me about that—and I think comforting in the same way I was talking about before, the way a smell might be comforting—something baking, or freshly mowed grass, something that brings you back to the place where you began. I want him to have that, and I don't think I will care if he rejects it. But I would regret not having given it to him in the first place.

ELLE: What would you tell your younger self about all of this—the questions of life?

DS: *Devotion* is my second memoir. *Slow Motion*, my first memoir, was the story of a pretty massive rebellion on my part, of my very lost younger self. I was in my early thirties writing about my early twenties, so there was this way of seeing my younger self from enough of a distance to have perspective but also not to feel that I had to protect myself. My dreams for myself then would have undersold me in a way. They were based on images and fantasies rather than any kind of real perspective. I spoke at a college where the whole freshman class had read *Slow Motion*, and I was so aware that they were looking at me in front of them, thinking, How did that girl become you? I could read it on their faces: How is that possible? That girl should be dead or just in some other universe. That girl's idea of a good time was not going to be sitting in a lotus position on her bedroom floor examining life. And yet if I could say anything to that girl, it's just, "Hold on." ⌒

Writing *Devotion*

WHEN I FINISHED WRITING *DEVOTION*, I felt bereft. I am often at loose ends when I come to the end of a novel or any long piece of work, but this time felt different: an aimlessness, a gray pall settled over me. I couldn't shake it. It was summer, and I spent part of each day, as I had during the years I worked on the book, practicing yoga, sitting in meditation. I continued to read classic (and not-so-classic) spiritual texts. I took walks, long drives, spent time with family and friends. But still this feeling would return. It took a while, but I finally realized what was happening: I was bereft because I still wanted to be writing—and living—this story.

I had no way of knowing, when I first had the daunting idea that I wanted to write a memoir about a personal search for meaning, that I would embark on a journey that would genuinely change me. I don't mean this in any grand, cue-the-violins kind of way, but rather, that my interior life would shift in subtle but profound ways, altering something as fundamental as the way I see the world. When I first began writing, my editor called me one morning with a question: *Do you think you're going to find answers?* I wasn't sure what she was hoping I would say, so it was with some trepidation that I responded truthfully: *No,* I said. *I want to live inside the questions.*

Though answers were not what I was looking for, I did learn some very important lessons—lessons that border on answers—during the course of writing *Devotion.*

> My editor called me one morning with a question: *Do you think you're going to find answers?* . . . I responded truthfully: *No.*

I approached each day, each moment, with a sense of openness to the idea that it had something to teach me. I said yes, rather than no, to experiences and people that I might have resisted in the past. When I began the book, it was with the instinct that everything I was looking for was within easy reach—essentially in my own backyard—and I had only to open my eyes and be willing to see. This turned out to be revelatory, and true. Sylvia Boorstein, Burt Visotzky, Stephen Cope—I did not go searching the world for these extraordinary teachers. They were revealed to me simply by my own willingness to show up.

For years, I had wanted to be someone who regularly meditates. I had a sense that sitting quietly—for two or five or ten minutes every day—was key to a sense of inner peace. But I was also convinced that I needed to be able to do meditation properly (whatever that entailed). I thought that my mind needed to be blank, a slate wiped clean. I was sure that if I caught myself thinking, it meant I was somehow doing it wrong. In fact, I learned from some of the best meditation teachers in the world that we all think— *all the time*—and that sitting in meditation allows us to see our thoughts, and to be kind and compassionate to ourselves about them. *Thinking, thinking*. And then simply coming back to the breath, again and again. Such a simple idea, and yet so radical: compassion for oneself.

I didn't know that I would get to know my parents better through the writing of this book. My father has been gone for half my life now; my mother, for seven years. And still, my relationship with them continues. I have learned and ▶

> 66 Sitting in meditation allows us to see our thoughts, and to be kind and compassionate to ourselves about them. 99

Writing *Devotion* (*continued*)

understood more about who they were as human beings, what made them tick. In particular, I have a greater understanding of why religious ritual was so important to my father. It gave shape and meaning to his days. It was a meditation of sorts for him, the Hebrew prayers he recited each morning a mantra, no different, really, than the intention that I bring to my yoga practice, or to meditation, or to the synagogue services I now attend with my family. *I am trying to do better*, is really all it is. *I am focusing on what is important.* As for my mother, my relationship with her had been difficult and painful for both of us. She had been so bitterly angry for most of my life. But in writing this book, I began to think about the fact that my mother had agreed to become observant and follow the rules and rituals of Orthodox Judaism in order to marry my father, who was an Orthodox Jew. My mother wasn't a believer—in fact, a friend described her to me as an atheist. How does someone make peace with the fact that she has chosen to live in a way she doesn't believe?

After *Devotion* was published, I was often asked: *So what answers do you now give your son?* At first I was taken aback by this question, and yet of course it was at the heart of what readers wanted to know. It was at the heart of what I wanted to know when I began searching! *What do we believe, Mommy?* But I never intended to supply Jacob with an answer, ready-made, prepackaged. Instead, what I hoped to do—and hope I have done—is supply him with a mother who has thought deeply about the questions. Who is open to talking about all of it, any time. Before I wrote *Devotion*, the subject of faith was radioactive for me. I was frightened, resistant, dismissive. Now Jacob regularly brings up his own spiritual thoughts and ideas because he's comfortable doing so—he knows it isn't scary or off-limits. He also knows that I won't dismiss his ideas, or tell him he's wrong, or that we do things *just because*—as I was told as a child.

One of my favorite moments in this book takes place when someone asks Sylvia Boorstein why she complicates her Buddhism with her Judaism. *Buddhism is so pure and simple—why complicate it?* And Sylvia answers by saying, *Because I* am *complicated with my Judaism. It's where I come from.* The idea that we're all complicated by the way we were raised—whether Jewish, Catholic, Muslim, Mormon, *whatever*—is something I've seen up close in the many letters and conversations I've had with readers of *Devotion*. We're complicated by where we come from, and part of our job, spiritually speaking, is to make peace with that—and not, as Stephen Cope says, throw the baby out with the bathwater. As Steve says, *There's still a baby in there.* Which leads me to the final and perhaps greatest lesson I learned in writing this memoir.

I used to have a secret, and secretly judgmental, belief that people who created spiritual lives for themselves, taking a little bit of wisdom from one religion or teacher or text and a little bit from another, were nothing more than spiritual dabblers, intellectually lazy seekers of easy solace. I've come to see that a spiritual life can be built—and, in fact, that the genuine building of a spiritual life is a rigorous discipline, no less valid for the breadth of its sources. Some of the smartest, most thoughtful people I have encountered have done precisely this and see no contradiction in it. Recently, a woman in the front row of an audience asked me how I would define myself. *I'm a meditating, Jewish yogi*, I answered. She rolled her eyes—I mean, she *really* rolled her eyes. And do you know what? I'm okay with that. I am building a path that feels genuine and relevant—connected both to my heritage and to other practices and pieces of wisdom that resonate with me. I hope that path continues to grow and evolve over many years.

A book about seeking reaches a point at which it must end, but with any luck the seeking continues. Many months after I finished the *Devotion*, I was on the phone one evening with Sylvia Boorstein. I was about to appear on a national television show, and I was nervous.

"It's okay, sweetheart," said Sylvia. "This is what you know now. That's all."

This is what you know now. Another moment in a string of revelatory moments. I can only know what I know now. That's all any of us can know. Hopefully, we'll know more an hour from now. And tonight. And tomorrow. And next year. But in the meantime, I wrote a book about what I know now. I know more than when I began it—and some day, with any luck, I'll realize that I've learned plenty since then. Maybe it will turn out that I was wrong about some things. Or deluded. Or naïve. But it stands as a document and contains within it every last bit of what I once knew. ❧

Have You Read?
More by Dani Shapiro

SLOW MOTION

At twenty-three, Dani Shapiro was in the midst of a major rebellion against her religious upbringing. She had dropped out of college, was halfheartedly acting in television commercials, and was carrying on with an older married man when her life was changed, in an instant, by a phone call. Her parents had been in a devastating car accident. Neither was expected to survive. In her first memoir, Shapiro offers this powerful true story of a life turned around—not by miracles or happy endings, but by unexpected personal catastrophe.

"Riveting. . . . A combination of breathtaking candor and bravado. . . . *Slow Motion* is a smart, well-written take on the form." —*San Francisco Chronicle*

"Absorbing, sweetly stinging. . . . Shapiro's book succeeds as a gracefully written story of reckoning inspired by tragedy and the long reach of familial roots."
—*Wall Street Journal*

"Fabulous." —*People*

"Shapiro does not sugarcoat her life; she writes with an eviscerating, raw honesty about the wrong turns and mistakes she made." —*Boston Globe*

Recommended Reading
Author's Picks

Happiness Is an Inside Job and *That's Funny, You Don't Look Buddhist* by Sylvia Boorstein. Actually, pretty much anything Sylvia Boorstein writes has a profound effect on me. She has a clarity of mind that makes its way seamlessly to the page.

Yoga and the Quest for the True Self by Stephen Cope. This is a page-turner of yoga metaphysics, with the added bonus of being full of wonderful literary references. Cope is a yogi and a scholar.

Buddha by Karen Armstrong is a beautifully written philosophical biography of the Buddha.

The Sabbath by Abraham Joshua Heschel. This brief, powerful book illuminated the significance and beauty of the Sabbath for me.

Gift from the Sea by Anne Morrow Lindbergh is an exquisite little book, perfectly structured.

For the Time Being by Annie Dillard. I love everything Dillard writes, but this book in particular gave me permission to write *Devotion* and showed me that what I was attempting to do was possible.

Letters to a Spiritual Seeker by Henry David Thoreau, along with *Walden*, regularly reminds me of the power and necessity of quiet reflection, as does Thomas Merton's *Thoughts in Solitude*.

Ambivalent Zen is a wonderful, irreverent memoir by Lawrence Shainberg about his lifelong relationship with meditation.

Do You Believe?: Conversations on God and Religion, a series of interviews ▶

conducted by Antonio Monda. Monda was able to get some very interesting people (ranging from Martin Scorcese to Grace Paley) to share their deepest thoughts about their spiritual and religious lives.

The Jew in the Lotus is Rodger Kamenetz's account of his historical trip with a delegation of Jewish leaders to visit the Dalai Lama in Dharmsala. A reported memoir, this book resides at the center of the intersection between Buddhism and Judaism.

Cutting Through Spiritual Materialism by Chogyam Trungpa is an elegant book about the dangers of an ego-driven spiritual life.

I would add here that the works of Jack Kornfield, Pema Chodron, and Sharon Salzberg sustained me during the writing of this book, and sustain me still. ⌒

Don't miss the next book by your favorite author. Sign up now for AuthorTracker by visiting www.AuthorTracker.com.